GREAT WOMEN IN CHRISTIAN HISTORY

# GREAT WOMEN
## *in*
## CHRISTIAN HISTORY

### 37 WOMEN WHO CHANGED THEIR WORLD

Editors

A. KENNETH CURTIS
DANIEL GRAVES

*Published by*

CHRISTIAN PUBLICATIONS, INC.
CAMP HILL, PENNSYLVANIA

*and*

Christian History Institute
WORCESTER, PENNSYLVANIA

CHRISTIAN PUBLICATIONS, INC.

3825 Hartzdale Drive, Camp Hill, PA 17011
www.christianpublications.com

*Faithful, biblical publishing since 1883*

*Great Women in Christian History*
ISBN: 0-88965-237-6
LOC Control Number: 2004114368
© 2004 by Christian History Institute
All rights reserved
Printed in the United States of America

04   05   06   07   08      5   4   3   2   1

*Note: Italicized words in Scripture
quotations are the emphasis of the author.*

# Contents

## Part 5: She Stooped to Conquer

## Part 6: Handicap? What Handicap?

## Part 7: First and Foremost

## Part 8: Mothering the World

## Part 9: Beyond Motherhood

# Preface

This is the first installation in an ongoing series of books to be published jointly by Christian Publications, Inc., and Christian History Institute. Both companies are located in eastern Pennsylvania, and we have discovered a common vision of producing books that tap into the priceless heritage of our Christian past and making these treasures accessible to the general reader who is not necessarily a specialist in church history.

This book-publishing venture is a natural extension of the mission of Christian History Institute. We were founded in 1982, and one of our major purposes was to provide research for historical Christian films that were produced by our sister companies, Gateway Films and Vision Video. As part of our film research efforts, we also prepared study guides and teacher's manuals, and this led to an experiment in providing a study guide in a magazine format. We called it *Christian History Magazine* and occasionally produced an issue when we had a new historical film around which to build it.

The magazine proved to have an appeal and an integrity of its own, and it soon developed into an ongoing quarterly publication that did not have to be linked to companion films. The reception of the magazine was gratifying, but we saw that it was more than we could handle if it was going to reach its fullest potential. So, an agreement was entered into with Christianity Today, Inc., a publisher of a dozen nationally prominent Christian magazines, whereby they would take over *Christian History* (now called *Christian History and Biography*).

In the meantime, some fifteen years ago, we recognized the need to reach an even broader "person-in-the-pew" audience than we could reach with the magazine, so we started a new publication called *Glimpses*, which was a church bulletin insert that was published twelve times a year. It provided accounts of great persons, issues and events from Christian history in a compelling story format that was easy to read and amply illustrated. That little publication started off as a two-color, two-page product and soon developed into a full-color, four-page publication that is now used by thousands of churches across many denominations.

One of the joys of publishing *Glimpses* was telling the often little-known but gripping stories of Christian women who played vital roles in the life of the Church and its mission over the centuries. This book is a compilation of many of the stories about women that were first published in *Glimpses*, as well as several additional original selections that were written especially for this volume.

Our work at Christian History Institute has always been so much of a team effort that it is difficult to know whom to thank and acknowledge. But, some people in particular have played special roles over the years in developing the content that has gone into this book. Most of the writing has been done by historian Dr. Diana Severance, author Randy Petersen and this book's editors, Dan Graves and Ken Curtis. We have been wonderfully supported by the research and picture editing of Ann Snyder and the publishing support of Beth Jacobson.

We send forth this first volume in our joint publishing venture with Christian Publications, Inc., with both awe and gratitude for the role women have played in building, nourishing and extending the Body of Christ over the ages. We trust that these stories will in some small way help to compensate for the recognition that so many women deserved but did not always receive. And, may it inspire Christian women today to see the high calling that God has so often uniquely bestowed upon His female servants.

It would, however, be a sad mistake to imply that this book is intended for women only. We are confident that many men cannot help but be inspired by the women in this book. We trust that it will lift their own sights in terms of obedience to God, courage and vision for Christ's kingdom.

In addition, there is another special audience that I have in mind and whom I pray will be inspired by these pages. I am referring to young girls ages ten to fourteen. We are all too well aware of the self-obsessed female role models foisted upon our young women by our culture. In these chapters, our daughters and granddaughters will find extraordinary women whose lives show another way, a most worthy and noble way, to live.

We are grateful for the privilege of sharing with you these unforgettable true stories. May they inspire you and spur you on to accomplish great things for the kingdom of God.

Dr. Ken Curtis
Founder and President
Christian History Institute

# Introduction

This book is about the lives of just thirty-seven notable Christian women out of the hundreds, even thousands, about whom we might have written. Christian history abounds with the names and records of women who easily could have been given a chapter in this book. And, as we well know, the names of even more notable Christian women have vanished unrecorded into the mists of history.

## The Horrors of History

Throughout history women have been downtrodden. Examples of codified cruelty to women, even within Christendom, are a dime a dozen. They have been sold as sex slaves, beaten, treated as plunder, burned as witches or saddled with the bulk of human work.

The Chinese practiced footbinding—a process that completely distorted women's foot bones and made walking excruciatingly painful for them—into the twentieth century. In the late Middle Ages, some Europeans began to encase women in chastity belts, which drove some wearers to suicide, if only to obtain sanitary relief. Hindus practiced *suttee*, the immolation of widows on funeral pyres, until it was stopped by British intervention in 1829. In many Muslim lands even today, women exist under the restrictions of a veil and are denied the right to claim an inheritance. The merciless practice of female circumcision is still practiced in a number of cultures. In parts of India and China, selective abortion that targets female babies has resulted in significant male/female imbalances in the population.

## Old Testament Women and Christ's Teaching

At the time and place of Jesus' birth, women were usually relegated to inferior status. Many men refused to even speak to their own wives in public! In the larger Roman Empire, matters were just as bad. Sexual morals were low, divorce was rife, polygamy was practiced and cult prostitution was commonplace. Hordes of women joined licentious mystery cults in an effort to slake their souls' thirst.

Jesus was steeped in the Law and the Prophets, which He revered as the Word of His heavenly Father, and He knew that there is scarcely a book in the Old Testament without a reference to women. The Jewish Scriptures cite the contributions of women more than the writings of any other world faith, and a few passages were even written by women, such as Miriam's song (see Exodus 15:20-21) and Hannah's prayer (see 1 Samuel 2:1-10).

A number of the women in the Bible played prominent roles, whether good or bad. There was Eve, who played a part in the fall of mankind (see Genesis 3). Miriam led the Israelites in song (see Exodus 15:20-21). Delilah trapped Samson (see Judges 16). Ruth demonstrated rare fidelity to her mother-in-law and became one of Jesus' ancestors (see the book of Ruth). Hannah prayed for a child and mothered the high priest Samuel (see 1 Samuel 1-2). Bathsheba bathed carelessly, and as a result David became forever an object lesson of the danger of the roving eye (see 2 Samuel 11-12). Michal scorned David and as a result bore no children, helping to free the throne for Solomon (see 2 Samuel 6:20-23).

Other biblical women's names are also memorable: Abigail, Athaliah, Deborah, Esther, Hagar, Jael, Jezebel, Leah, Rachel, Rahab, Rebekah, Sarah and Tamar. It is true that women are most often seen as childbearers and homemakers in the Scriptures, but these are not negligible roles. Perhaps that is why in the books of Kings and Chronicles, mothers of good (and bad) kings are often named. Motherly influence on successive generations is recognized as greatly important.

In light of this rich history of women in the Bible, Jesus accorded women great respect. He realized that women share the same essential relationship with God as do men, for when God created humans, He created both genders in His image and likeness. We should not be surprised, then, to find God's love likened to a mother's love in Isaiah 49:15. Likewise, the Bible makes no distinction between obedience to father or mother. Children are to honor and obey both (see Exodus 20:12), and the advice of mothers should not be ignored (see Proverbs 1:8).

Jesus picked up on these truths, which His contemporaries had often neglected, and He extended the teachings of the Old Testament to cover both men and women. For example, it was common practice that a man who engaged in premarital sex was not punished, but a woman could be (see Deuteronomy 22:13-20). Jesus, however, called both genders to holiness (see, for example, John 8:11). Inheritance laws favored men, and widows apparently could not inherit property, but Jesus rejected questions of inheritance (see Luke 12:13-21). In court, the testimony of two men established a matter, and women were usually not given the right to testify; Jesus turned women into witnesses for Him at His resurrection (see Matthew 28:10; Luke 24:22-24; John 20:18). Although divorce was entirely a man's prerogative under Jewish law, Jesus spoke as if women too could divorce men. However, He forbade divorce altogether except in cases of sexual infidelity, extending the thinking of the prophet Malachi, who, in Malachi 2:13-16, demanded that a man keep faith with his wife. Countless women have benefited from this injunction, for, historically, divorce has placed more of an economic disadvantage and social stigma on women than on men.

## Attitude Shines Through

Jesus' underlying attitudes did as much to elevate the status of women as what He said or did. He spoke openly to women and allowed them to publicly touch Him. His disciples marveled at this. When they found Him speaking to a woman at a well (a Samaritan, to boot), they were surprised (see John 4:1-42). And Jesus did not merely converse with the Samaritan woman but revealed to her what He had so far proclaimed to no one else—that He was the Messiah. She became one of His first evangelists, telling her whole village about Him. As a result, a number of Samaritans came to believe in Christ.

On another occasion Jesus granted a Syrophonecian woman a miracle after some lively repartee. When He declared that it was not right to give the food of children (the Jews) to dogs (the Gentiles), she retorted, "But even the dogs eat the crumbs that fall from their masters' table" (Matthew 15:27, NIV). He responded, "Woman, you have great faith! Your request is granted" (15:28, NIV). He was teaching His disciples the error of writing off Gentiles—and women—as unimportant in the kingdom of God.

When a woman with a hemorrhage touched the hem of Christ's garment (possibly making Him unclean under the law), He not only healed her issue of blood but freed her from her sins (see Luke 8:40-48).

None of Jesus' encounters with women can be called typical, but one exemplifies better than any other His manner with women. While eating at a Pharisee's house, Jesus allowed a woman with a "past" to touch Him. The Pharisees muttered, "If He was a prophet, He would know what sort of woman this is who touches Him," but Jesus rebuked them. He pointed out that whereas Simon the Pharisee, His host, had not offered Him the traditional foot washing or a greeting kiss, the woman had bathed His feet with tears, kissed them and wiped them with her hair. "Because her love is great, her sins which are many are forgiven her," He said (see Luke 7:36-50). Thus Jesus set a new standard of treatment for outcast women and directly met one woman's personal cry for acceptance and forgiveness.

## Christ Set Women Free

Jesus always met women according to their needs and individuality. He discipled them just the same as men: Mary sat at His feet to learn from Him (see Luke 10:39). And, He gave their very tears dignity. Two of the resurrections He performed were carried out because of His compassion for the grief of women (see Luke 7:11-16; John 11). And, it was women to whom Christ first revealed Himself after His resurrection; they then carried the news to the male disciples.

Not one derogatory word toward women can be found in all of Christ's relations with them. This is in stark contrast to the words of other religious greats. Consider, for instance, these words of the Buddha:

> Women are soon angered, Ananda; women are full of passion, Ananda; women are envious, Ananda; women are stupid, Ananda. That is the reason, Ananda—that [is] the cause—why women have no place in public assemblies, do not carry on business, and do not earn their living by any profession.

Christ, who said little about women, did more to ennoble them than any other person in history. Women in AD 25 desperately needed two of the gifts that He offered: righteousness and freedom. It is safe to say that those needs have not diminished even in our day, and it is apparent that those gifts have elevated women's conditions wherever the gospel of Christ has been planted.

## What About Paul?

The Apostle Paul has been accused of being anti-woman, principally because of his command that women remain silent in church (see 1 Corinthians 14:34-35). Yet Paul issued some of the most enlightened utterances ever made regarding women. For example, he wrote, "There is neither Jew nor Greek . . . male nor female, for you are all one in Christ Jesus" (Galatians 3:28, NIV). He taught men to love their wives as Christ loved the Church, even laying down their lives for them (see Ephesians 5:25-33). He taught that a man's body is owned by his wife and vice versa (see 1 Corinthians 7:4). The medieval ideal of male chivalry grew out of Paul's themes, and courtesy toward women, especially in the Victorian era, was an outgrowth of that earlier ideal.

Today, as our culture increasingly drifts away from Christian thinking, the idea of men treating women with courtesy is on the decline, and women are more and more viewed as either competitors or sex objects. Paul, however, often labored side by side with women, and his many meaningful and respected relationships with them are suggested by the salutations to and from them in his letters.

## The Influence of Women

Not surprisingly, because of Christ's example and Paul's teaching, women have had a tremendous influence on the spread of Christianity and indeed on the entire tone of civilization. They have served God's kingdom as martyrs, wives, mothers, writers, educators, missionaries, charitable workers and protesters, among other things. What follows is just a short list of some of the ways that women have accomplished great things for their own gender and for Christians in general.

## Women as Martyrs

Throughout Christian history women have suffered as martyrs, winning converts through their fervent testimonies. The courage of an ordinary slave girl, Blandina, inspired her fellow martyrs who were with her in the arena of Lyons, France, around AD 177. In North Africa around AD 200, Perpetua and Felicitas were fed to wild beasts after every possible plea and threat—including taking their newborn babies from them—had been made to persuade them to recant. The Himyarite martyrs of 523 in Arabian regions were predominantly women. One thousand years later, Anabaptist women such as Balthasar Hubmaier's wife were martyred alongside men. Waldensian and Huguenot women suffered indignities, torture and death for their faith. In other periods, women such as Mary Dyer, Agnes Askew and Edith Stein also became martyrs for their faith.

## Women as Wives

Untold numbers of Christian women have civilized savage men through marriage. We hear of only the famous cases, such as Queen Clothilde, who by converting her husband to Christ brought the Salic Franks into the Christian fold in 496. Queen Giselle, wife of St. Stephen of Hungary, played a role in the conversion of her Balkan nation in the tenth and eleventh centuries. At about the same time, Margaret of Scotland persuaded her husband, Malcolm, to engage in charitable works, and the sixth century's Queen Radegunde inspired conversions by her example of a holy life, first in the violent court of King Clothaire and later in an abbey. More recently, the influence of Mai-Ling Soong on her husband, Chiang Kai Shek, led not only to his conversion as a Methodist Christian but to efforts at social reform in China.

## Women as Writers

In the Dark Ages many women rose to prominence as writers. In the tenth century Hrotsvit von Gandersheim became Christianity's first known playwright. Sometime between 1373 and 1393, Julian of Norwich wrote the first book in English by a woman. Two centuries earlier, the German abbess Hildegard of Bingen had produced an encyclopedia. Even in our own era, the influence of women writers upon the Church has not been lacking. Hannah Smith helped hundreds of thousands with her book *A Christian's*

*Secret of a Happy Life*. Corrie Ten Boom's life story, *The Hiding Place*, has touched millions. Hannah More achieved fame as a playwright in the eighteenth century and, with her sisters, was a driving force in the early Sunday school movement. Many of the Church's best-loved hymns were penned by Fanny Crosby.

## Women as Charitable Workers

Part of the reason Christianity spread so quickly was that it taught compassion. We read in Acts 9 that Dorcas sewed clothes for the poor (see 9:36-43), and this was but the beginning of a trend. The Church cared for widows and the elderly; it produced hospitals, leper houses, soup lines and more. Charity on the Christian scale had been previously unknown among the pagans of Europe, and Christian women were at the head of the charity movement. Illustrious organizers of charitable operations in Christianity's early days were Fabiola, Melania and Paula. In the Middle Ages, Elizabeth of Hungary won herself a lasting name because of her concern for lepers. Nearer to our own time, Caroline Chisholm showed the power of a woman to reform a cruel immigration system, and the Quaker Elizabeth Fry spearheaded prison reform.

## Women as Protesters

The pages of our nation's history teem with the names of women who have brought about positive change through their refusal to stay silent. Women such as Mary Ashton Livermore and Frances Willard led the temperance movement at a time when male drunkenness had made the lives of many women miniature hells. Harriet Beecher Stowe was but the most visible Christian woman in the war for the abolition of slavery—Harriet Tubman battled in the trenches while Stowe battled from her desk.

## America Has Had Its Share of Christian Notables

Christian women have actively contributed not just to Christendom as a whole but also to the American story in particular. Anne Hutchinson, for example, was in many ways the prototype for other women who would later fight for women's concerns. Abigail Adams, wife of one president and mother to another, was a woman of faith. Hannah Adams was the first American woman to make a living from her writing. Anne Bradstreet of Massachusetts was the first woman to have a volume of poetry published in the English tongue, and Pulitzer prize-winning novelist Frances Parkinson Keyes made no bones about her faith. The first practical techniques for preserving food in transport were contrived by the Quaker Mary Engle Pennington. Prominent educators included Mary McLeod Bethune, and a quarter-century before Vassar opened its doors, Mary Lyon brought the female training center Mount Holyoke College into existence. Joni Eareckson Tada's triumphant response to an accident that made her a quadriplegic has encouraged thousands facing similar distress. Christian women in America have been a glory to their nation and to the world as they strode onto the world stage as missionaries, educators and doctors.

## Christian Women Benefit Themselves

The Body of Christ has never treated women perfectly. For example, seventy-five percent of those who perished in witch trials between 1484 and 1782 were women. The Church of Christ has never claimed to be perfect. It has always been made up of both redeemed sinners and opportunists, whom Christ identified as wolves in sheep's clothing (see Matthew 7:15). There is no denying its flaws, its times of regression and aberration from the gospel and its inhumane treatment of those within and without its fellowship. At the same time, history reveals a significant growth in the understanding of and profound appreciation for the role of women in the Church and society over the years.

As the case studies in this book so clearly demonstrate, the good that the Church has brought to this earth cannot be understood apart from the essential role that women have played. It is important to recognize and remember the women in this book and many others like them, not only to give them credit for the good they have done, but to encourage the women of today and tomorrow to strive onward and continue to fulfill their indispensable and vital role in the kingdom of God.

# Part 1
## It's a (Wo)man's World

*The Lord used them
to accomplish what
no man had.*

# A MOSES
## *to*
# HER PEOPLE

*The boatman eyed the pair of black women suspiciously. "You just stand aside, you two; I'll attend to your case by and by." Inwardly, the women trembled. They knew that their forged pass could not withstand close scrutiny.*

*Harriet Tubman led young, terrified Tilly to the bow of the boat where no one else was standing. There she knelt, fixed her eyes on the water and groaned a prayer. "Oh, Lord! You've been wid me in six troubles; don't desert me in the seventh!" She continued to pray as Tilly's panic mounted.*

*Finally, the boatman came over and touched Harriet on the shoulder. Tilly thought the game was up. She would be returned to the South where she would endure a whipping and a forced marriage. Harriet would go to prison or be burned at the stake—the death one friend had predicted for her. But the boatman said, "You can come now and get your tickets." The women breathed inward sighs of relief.*

## Harriet Tubman

**Born:** Around 1820 or '21 in Dorchester County, MA

**Education:** No formal education

**Married:** John Tubman in 1844

**Children:** None

**Died:** March 10, 1913, in Auburn, NY

**Quote:** "Her prayer was the prayer of faith and she expected an answer."

## Adversity Served Its Purpose

Harriet Tubman was a slave who escaped to freedom and became a "conductor" on the Underground Railroad. Over the course of her work with the Railroad, she delivered over 300 runaway slaves into freedom in the northern United States and Canada. In fact, she was so successful that a $40,000 reward was offered for her capture, dead or alive.

*Two years after her own escape from slavery, Harriet Tubman returned to rescue her husband and found him living with another woman. She didn't falter in the face of this discouraging blow. Instead, she went on to bring more slaves out of the South via the Underground Railroad than any other "conductor."*

Harriet was born around 1820 on a plantation in Maryland. Her given name was Araminta, but around the time of her marriage to John Tubman in 1844, she took her mother's name, Harriet.

If Harriet had been treated kindly as a slave, she might have never attempted the feats for which she is famous. But vicious masters and mistresses forced her to perform tasks that were almost beyond human endurance, and as a result, once she had gained her own freedom, she determined to help others escape their horrible bondage as well.

One mistress, who rented young Harriet from her owner for only a pittance, forced Harriet to work both night and day. By day she cleaned and cooked, and by night she rocked the mistress's baby so the mistress could sleep in peace. A lash was at hand in case Harriet fell asleep and the baby cried, and there were scars on Harriet's neck to prove that the whip was often employed. As a result of the extremely hard labor, Harriet's body broke down, and she was returned to her owner, exhausted and starving. Her mother nursed her back to health.

When she had recovered a little, Harriet's master rented her out to a farmer who made her lift and haul heavy burdens. If she failed, she was flogged. Over time she developed strong muscles because of this work, and in the future, strong men would marvel at her feats of strength. Yet once again her body broke down and she was returned to her owner. After she recovered, she was rented out to several other masters until her eventual escape.

When she was about thirteen years old, an overseer cracked Harriet's skull when he flung a two-pound weight at a disobedient slave. She fell into a stupor and was taken to her bed, where she wasted away to almost nothing. Once again her mother nursed her. As a result of the blow to her head, Harriet suffered bouts of uncontrollable sleepiness—which made her appear to be stupid—until the end of her life. Behind the appearance of laziness and stupidity, however, was a keen mind.

Although difficult, the hardships Harriet faced served a purpose in her life. Through the first experience she learned to go without food and sleep when she had to, which benefited her greatly during the long nights when she guided other slaves to freedom. She herself insisted that the cruelty of her mistress served to prepare her for the rescues that made her name legendary. And the strength she gained through the second experience helped her years later when she saved a slave from capture by dragging him out of a sheriff's office and carrying him to safety against the resistance of the sheriff and his deputies. Through all of the adversity Harriet faced, God was preparing her for something big.

## A Prayer She Regretted

Harriet would not have become a Moses to her people if God had not been with her. She was at first a surly child, but she was raised to fear God, and she learned at a young age to call upon the Lord for help at any hour of the day or night.

Harriet often prayed for her master, "Oh, dear Lord, change dat man's heart and make him a Christian." But, when she heard that she was to be sent to a chain gang in the far South, she changed her prayer: "Lord, if you ain't never going to change dat man's heart, kill him, Lord, and take him out of de way, so he won't do no more mischief."

The master died suddenly, as wickedly as he had lived. Brokenhearted and full of guilt, Harriet began to pray without ceasing. In her own words, "Den it 'peared like I would give de world full of silver and gold, if I had it, to bring that pore soul back, I would give myself; I would give eberyting! But he was gone, I couldn't pray for him no more." When she washed, she asked to be washed white of sin. When she swept, she pleaded to be swept clean in her soul.

## "Hain't Got No Friend but You"

Christian mystics claim that God can communicate directly with a heart that is in touch with

*I grew up like a neglected weed—ignorant of liberty, having no experience of it. I was not happy or contented: every time I saw a white man I was afraid of being carried away. I had two sisters carried away in a chain gang—one of them left two children. We were always uneasy. Now I've been free, I know what slavery is. I have seen hundreds of escaped slaves but I never saw one who was willing to go back and be a slave. I have no opportunity to see my friends in my native land [the South]. We would rather stay in our native land if we could be as free there as we are here. I think slavery is the next thing to hell. If a person would send another into bondage he would, it appears to me, be bad enough to send him to hell if he could.*

*—Harriet Tubman*

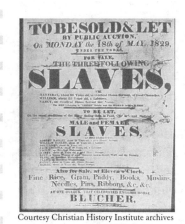

Courtesy Christian History Institute archives

*A slave poster*

Him. Harriet may not have known what a mystic was, but she seemed to be able to hear the Lord's voice. In 1849, in some mysterious way that she could not fully explain, He warned her to flee northward. She urged her brothers to join her.

Together they started north toward freedom, but the men soon fell away out of fear of the consequences if they were caught. Harriet went on alone. Traveling at night, she fixed her eyes on the North Star, and during the day she hid. Like the revolutionary orator Patrick Henry, she knew she was entitled to liberty or death. If she could not be free, then she vowed not to be taken alive but to fight with all her strength. Guided by God and assisted by an almost superhuman cunning, she successfully escaped.

When she arrived in the North, she found herself alone. There was no one to help her and no one she knew to share her joy—they all remained behind in slavery. "Oh, how I prayed den, lying on de cold, damp ground, 'Oh, dear Lord, I hain't got no friend but you. Come to my help, Lord, for I'm in trouble!' " Harriet came to a solemn resolution: She would make a home for her family in the North and, with the Lord's help, bring them there.

## *"I Nebber Run My Train off de Track"*

Harriet chose to look not at her loss but at the opportunity in front of her. Instead of clinging to security, she would use her contacts and hard-won knowledge to bring others to freedom. Night and day she worked, saving pennies, and when she had enough money, she slipped away from her home to rescue slaves and pilot them north. When the strength of men failed and they wanted to turn back, she pulled out her revolver and fiercely warned them, "Dead niggers tell no tales; you go on or die!" Invariably, they went on.

Nineteen times, Harriet, bold to the point of brazenness, ventured into the South. She experienced many narrow escapes, but the Lord always sent help.

Once, a "premonition" warned Harriet that she must immediately turn aside from the path she was walking on and cross a swollen stream. Not knowing the depth of the river, the men who were with her hung back, but Harriet stepped boldly into the water and found that it never came above her chin. When the men saw that she was safely across, they followed her. Later, Harriet learned that a party had been waiting farther down the path to seize them. If it had not been for the whisper of warning in Harriet's mind, they would have been captured.

Another time, the Lord warned Harriet that her parents were in special danger. She felt that she was to go to a certain house and ask for $20. The owner of the house told her that the Lord had sent her to the wrong place, but Harriet would not budge. She drifted asleep, waking only long enough to insist that she wasn't leaving until she got the money. Visitors passing through the busy house spread her story and collected $60 for her. Her father, it turned out, was facing criminal charges for helping runaway slaves, and the money was needed to transport him to Canada.

*Three years before the Emancipation Proclamation officially freed the slaves, Harriet Tubman had a vision of her people being liberated. She was so full of joy that she couldn't eat! When the proclamation was finally issued on January 1, 1863, she did not rejoice like everyone else. "I did my rejoicing three years ago," she said.*

Yet another time some friends of hers found Harriet sleeping in a park beneath a notice offering a reward for her capture! (She couldn't read.) Harriet had to lie wet in swamps and bury herself in potato fields, but deliverance always came, sometimes through a friend on the Underground Railroad and sometimes by her own wits.

Harriet always gave the Lord the credit. As biographer Sarah Bradford wrote,

> Sudden deliverance never seemed to strike her as at all mysterious; her prayer was the prayer of faith and she expected an answer. . . . When surprise was expressed at her courage and daring, or at her unexpected deliverance, she would always reply: "Don't, I tell you, Missus, 'twasn't me, 'twas de Lord!"

Thanks to Him, Harriet could declare, "On my underground railroad, I nebber run my train off de track and I never los' a passenger."

## The Civil War and After

During the Civil War, Harriet scouted for the Union army and walked the battlefields unscathed while gunshots fell like hail. With songs and cheerful words, she coaxed slaves, who were as afraid of the Yankees as they were of their own masters, to reveal important information to her. She nursed wounded soldiers, even those with deadly diseases that she might catch. She was not paid for her efforts, and Congress later jeered at an attempt to award her a pension. Consequently, Harriet was impoverished in her old age.

She died on March 10, 1913, in Auburn, New York. Throughout her life, Harriet's spirit remained unquenchable, and the God she trusted did not disappoint her. Her life is a powerful example of step-by-step trust in the Lord.

*Recommended reading: Sarah H. Bradford,* Harriet Tubman: The Moses of Her People *(New York: Corinth, 1961).*

# PERSEVERING
## *in*
# ISOLATION

Courtesy W.P. Livingstone, *Christina Forsyth of Fingoland* (New York: George H. Doran, 1919)

*C*hristina Moir could only suppose that she had been jilted. She had reached an understanding with a banker's son who attended the same Presbyterian church in Glasgow, Scotland, as she did. The plan was that he would spend a few years in India, then return to Scotland to make her his wife. Christina and her two sisters were asked to correspond with him, and they happily obliged. Soon, letters found their way into the post. Christina's sisters received responses, but she did not. She waited in vain for a reply. Letters continued to pass between the two other Moir girls and the banker's son, but none came for Christina. Gradually, all reference to her was dropped from his letters to her sisters. Christina was crushed.

## Christina Forsyth

**Born:** October 23, 1844, in Glasgow, Scotland
**Education:** No college or university education
**Married:** Allan Forsyth around 1884
**Children:** None
**Died:** 1918 in Scotland
**Quote:** *"I have done very little. I should like to do much more before I die."*

At such a moment, an ordinary woman might indulge in self-pity or bitterness or seek solace in another romance. Christina, however, charted a different course. Years earlier, when she was fourteen, a visiting cousin had asked her if she had faith in Christ. Although reared in a Christian home and drilled in the catechism, Christina had never put that question to herself. That same evening she heard a workman tell how he had come to Christ, and his testimony so impressed her that she returned home to kneel by her bedside and settle the question for herself once and for all.

Christina was determined to overcome her heartache by keeping God in sight. She wrote a long poem about His sufferings and viewed hers through the prism of His: "Here night shuts out the day/ 'Earth's fairest flow'rs bloom but to fade and die.'/ And fond-

17

Courtesy W.P. Livingstone, *Christina Forsyth of Fingoland* (New York: George H. Doran, 1919)

*Fingo women*

*est friends forsake. He felt this too./ Cling close to Him; He will not leave in life/ Nor yet in death foresake."*

## Her Life Not Her Own

A few years before, Christina might have turned to drawing or painting when she experienced rejection, but her father believed that those were not useful subjects for a woman to practice, so he forbade them. She was his second daughter and a serious young woman. When she was only ten years old, her mother, who had taught Christina Scripture, died. Her mother had rejoiced that she would soon see Jesus face-to-face. Christina's father had married late in life and died when she was twenty. But even at twenty-eight, no longer under her father's orders and apparently jilted, she was still not her own mistress. Her brother, John, having completed his training for the ministry, was assigned a church. As a single man, he needed someone to keep house for him, so Christina moved to his manse at Cairneyhill, near Dunfermline. She acted as his hostess and was a tireless worker among the people of her brother's congregation.

At some time in the mid-1870s, Christina met Allan Forsyth, a mining engineer, when he traveled to Scotland from Australia to visit his aunt. He was impressed by Christina's cheerful and helpful spirit. He proposed to her, and Christina accepted. Before they could marry, however, he had work to do in South America, and so he departed. Both understood that there was to be a wait of several years before they would be married.

## A Volunteer at Her Own Expense

When her brother John married, Christina was no longer needed at the manse. She applied to the Presbyterian mission as an unpaid volunteer, offering to support herself from a small inheritance. To her surprise, the board accepted her, and in 1879 she sailed for Africa on the S.S. *Nubian*. She was thirty-four.

Twenty-four days later, she arrived at Cape Town. Soon after, she reached East London, South Africa, her port of destination, but she was unable to disembark due to a storm. The next day she was swung over the side of the ship in a basket and lowered to land. She was an absolute stranger on the continent.

She found a room in a hotel, and the next day she was rescued by a friendly steamship agent who served the Church by helping its missionaries. He arranged for her passage inland, and she was assigned to the mission station at Emgwali, where she worked as a school assistant to Miss Ogilvie, listening to South African children recite their phonics: "*Ba, be, bo . . .*"

Then one of the missionaries at the Paterson station, Mrs. Davidson, fell ill, and Christina transferred there to lend her assistance. She found the two-day trip to be a delight. Fourteen oxen hauled her wagon across the rain-washed land, which was dotted with geraniums and aloe. She camped in "gypsy fashion" that night.

Upon her arrival, the Davidsons counted Christina a godsend. She was energetic and persevered at any task that was assigned to her. Despite the Zulu wars in which churches and missions were being burned around them, the Davidsons and Christina refused to flee.

In her three years at Paterson, Christina mastered the village's South African language, which is quite difficult because of its many clicking sounds. For their part, the Africans could not pronounce "Moir" and instead named her "Moyana," meaning "a breath" or "a little breeze."

## "Thy Maker Is Thy Husband"

Finally, in 1884 it was time for Christina to depart for Scotland for her wedding to Allan Forsyth. Everyone in Paterson was sad to see her go.

The banker's son, who had jilted her, was now settled in Glasgow, and when he learned of Christina's imminent wedding, he traveled to see her. He asked her why she hadn't written to him, and they came to realize that their letters to one another had been intercepted by a jealous admirer. The banker's son had suffered as greatly as Christina herself from the cruel trick. Despite this revelation, Christina kept her commitment to Allan Forsyth and they married.

Allan and Christina Forsyth did not remain in Scotland. Allan was determined to make his fortune in the Transvaal gold mines in Africa, so the newlyweds settled at Lydenburg, South Africa. Less than a year later, in 1885, an elder of their church pressed a piece of paper into Christina's hand. "Thy maker is thy husband," it read (see Isaiah 54:5). Allan was dead. His saddle had slipped as he forded the swollen Komati River, and he had been swept into the torrent and drowned.

The banker's son offered Christina a home with his sisters, but she did not care to be obligated to him. She still had her income of £40 a year and, determined to offer herself

*Christina Forsyth had asked for the hardest job that could be found. What was the outcome of her work? Here are some examples: Mazawazi, the most hardened woman in Xolobe, became a Christian in a tribe in which no church had been able to survive; her neighbors marveled at the change in her. John Mbanga, a drunkard, reformed and became a bold preacher. Gungubele turned to Christ after his beloved daughter died; he won twenty-seven of his relatives to Christ and became the alternate preacher at the church in Xolobe.*

again as a missionary, she wrote to the board, insisting that she would serve at her own expense and did not want to displace another missionary. Her offer was immediately accepted, and in 1886 she returned to help the Davidsons.

Christina, however, was no longer content to merely assist. She wanted a definite bit of work that she could call her own and for which she herself would be responsible. She suggested that they send her to the most "backward" region in South Africa. Half in jest, Mr. Davidson mentioned Xolobe.

"Send me there," said Christina.

"They are lazy, liars and notorious thieves," said Mr. Davidson. "Again and again I have tried, and again and again, on account of the opposition, I have had to close the school and leave the place to itself. It would never do for you to go there alone."

"I will go at once," asserted Christina. She knew that Mr. Davidson was not exaggerating. Christians called the Xolobe "wolves." Only one Xolobe had ever become a Christian and kept his faith.

## A Tough Job to Call Her Own

When, later in 1886, Christina arrived between the sharp hills that flanked the villages of Xolobe, she thought that perhaps she had overcommitted herself after all. The people were either apathetic or openly hostile toward her. They lived for beer binges and sexual orgies. There was no sign of Mr. Davidson's previous work among them, and the challenge appeared to be impossible. Where would she even begin?

In that moment, the Lord gave Christina the promise of Ezekiel 36:36: "The heathen that are left round about you shall know that I the LORD build the ruined places, and plant that that was desolate: I the LORD have spoken it, and I will do it."

Christina offered schooling to the people in Xolobe, and she walked from village to village attempting to tell them about Christ. In many instances, she found the adults gone, indulging in drunken orgies, so she sat down with the hungry children in the huts and taught them about Jesus. She visited the sick and took cast-out children into her own home.

Her work was not without its dangers. One time, as she was returning home in the dark, she lost her way and could finally go no farther. She lay down on the hillside where she was, and in the morning she woke to find herself on the edge of a precipice. If she had taken one more step, she would have plunged to her death.

Another time, death or worse stared her in the face when two thugs fell into step before and behind her as she walked along a path. Only the sudden appearance of a shepherd in the hills above saved her.

The hardships of life in Xolobe seemed unending, and the progress was invisible. Chief Mnyila opposed Christina and forbade his people to attend her meetings. He arranged parties to distract those who were leaning toward Christianity, and once he even sent his brother to tell Christina that the village would be glad to see her gone. His relentless opposition kept many people from Christ; few men cared to lose their status in the tribe by embracing a foreign faith.

Christina's persistence succeeded in obtaining permission for a few children to attend her school, but the first lad who was converted to Christianity was handed over to the witch doctor to be tormented until he renounced the faith.

Courtesy W.P. Livingstone, *Christina Forsyth of Fingoland* (New York: George H. Doran, 1919)

*Xolobe, the rugged terrain where Christina worked*

Christina was lonely. She had worked alone with the Xolobe for several years before an assistant, Isabella Lamb, was sent to her, but Isabella soon left because the work was too hard and discouraging. Isabella went on to do good work in a South African hospital; meanwhile, Christina toiled on alone. At one time, fever threatened to close the school. At another time, a tax miffed the villagers and all the pupils were withdrawn from the school. At other times, pupils were pulled from their classes because someone had become a Christian. Christina's pupils did not escape harrassment, either. Some were scourged; some had their clothes and wages stolen. But amazingly, considering the obstacles, Christina witnessed fifty conversions to Christianity by 1899.

Courtesy W.P. Livingstone, *Christina Forsyth of Fingoland* (New York: George H. Doran, 1919)

*Christina as an elderly woman*

A church building was needed to accommodate the new Christians, and plans were made to build one. But, just when the building was completed, it burned to the ground. "There is only one thing to do; we must build another," said Christina calmly.

The dedication of the second church seemed to wake Xolobe from its slumber. Many came to hear a native evangelist speak, and revival broke out. By Christina's 10th year at Xolobe, 117 natives had been baptized.

## She Wanted to Win the World

Year after year, Christina plodded on. She was always merry, but eventually she began to show signs of wear. Her heart began to fail, and she developed rheumatism, which she thought was punishment from God because she had accepted a salary to pay for a servant. Her correspondents had to gently remind her that such disease was the natural outcome of a life spent working under harsh conditions.

Despite all that she had accomplished, Christina was dissatisfied with what she had done, for she was eager to see all of Africa—and the whole world—won for Christ. At the age of seventy she read of Mary Slessor's mission work in Calabar and was inspired to work harder. But the strength she needed was no longer there, and in 1916 it was time for her to retire from the mission field.

In spite of her failing health, Christina dreaded her return to Scotland. She was sure that thirty years away from civilization had made her unfit for society. She steeled herself for the ordeal by reminding herself that the same Christ stood with her who had been her stronghold when she was "jilted," who had kept her foot on the precipice and comforted her in African isolation. In the last months of her life, Christina told her biographer that she would give the thirty years of her life to Xolobe all over again if she were given the chance. She died in 1918.

*Recommended reading: W.P. Livingstone,* Christina Forsyth of Fingoland *(New York: George H. Doran, 1919).*

# EXPLORERS
## *of*
## *the* GOBI

*W*hen we envision middle-aged Victorian missionary women, we generally don't picture them sliding down sandhills. But intrepid adventurers Eva and Francesca French and Mildred Cable were only too happy to experiment.

> We were told to slide down the sandhills propelling ourselves by movements of our hands. This we found to be a very simple and effective way of descent, as the whole warm dry surface moved with us. At a certain point a loud, clear vibrating sound responded to our movements, resembling the twang of a mighty musical instrument, which sound seemed to proceed from the very center of the hill.

The geographical societies back home would want to hear about this mystery of the Gobi Desert!

## The China Trio

**Born:** *Eva, 1869 in Algeria; Francesca, December 12, 1871, in Bruges, Belgium; Mildred, February 21, 1878, in Guildford, England*
**Education:** *Attended colleges or universities*
**Married:** *Did not marry*
**Children:** *None*

*(cont'd on next page)*

## The China Trio

That the "China Trio" were even in the Gobi was a mystery in itself. Dozens of Chinese Christians in Hwodjou, where they had been living, had raised their voices imploring "Grey Lady," "Brown Lady" and "Blue Lady," as the Chinese called them, to stay with them. Regretfully, the three greying women had touched the hands that stretched out to them but nonetheless climbed into their waiting rickshaws. Their hearts were sad, for, as they wrote, "to say 'goodbye' is to die a little." And yet all three felt the lilt of adventure in

# The China Trio

**Died:** *Eva, July 8, 1960, in Shaftesbury, Dorset, England; Francesca, August 2, 1960, in London; Mildred, April 30, 1952, in London*

**Quote:** *"We have proved the truth of Christ's words 'Lo, I am with you always even unto the end of the world.' We have known joy unspeakable as men and women came from darkness into the light and from the power of Satan unto God."*

their veins. Where were they going? They did not know. They knew only that God was calling them to some work in China's remote northwest.

They also did not know the ordeals they would soon face. Before their adventure was over, they would endure hunger, thirst, pain and sleeplessness; they would be robbed, arrested by a warlord and stoned. They would live lives of grueling adventure and make journeys that no other European woman had made before.

## Eva

Evangeline French was the oldest of the three women. She was born in 1869 in Algeria, and in her youth she was both daring and rebellious. And, for reasons that she could not explain, she was angry. She vented her rage by getting into escapades, cracking her head, falling into the fire and tumbling into ponds.

One day Eva exploded to her amiable sister Francesca, "If I could take upon myself the world's misery, I would—and jump into the sea with it."

"Eva, there is no need to do that. It was done long ago, on the cross," responded Francesca.

Her sister's reply sobered Eva. Two weeks later, she slipped into a chapel, sought the presence of Christ and began to change. She spoke to the vicar at the chapel, and he gave her work to do.

After completing her education in Geneva, Eva applied to work as a missionary with the China Inland Mission. In 1893, at the age of twenty-four, she left for China, where she was assigned to the Shansi mission. She was there when the Boxer Rebellion broke out. With the support of the empress dowager, the Boxers sought to fling foreign influences out of China. In Shansi Province, where Eva worked, 700 Christians, including 50 missionaries, were butchered.

Eva obtained a pass and fled toward the treaty port of Hankow, which was held by Western powers. A party of Boxers overtook her cart, and a man seized her by the hair and raised his sword to kill her. At that moment, a box of silver spilled out of the cart. The attacker let go of Eva to grab the loot, and Eva was free.

She returned to England, but twelve months later she was on her way back to China. She took Mildred Cable with her.

## Mildred

Mildred was born in England, the daughter of a draper. As a young woman she had heard a missionary speaker tell of China's spiritual need, and since then she had been eager to serve as a missionary. She studied nursing and chemistry, sure that healing hands and practical skills would open doors of witness for her.

During her school years, she was engaged to a young man who seemed as willing to go to China as she was. One day, however, he wrote to her and said that their relationship was over if she insisted on following her dream. Mildred insisted, and the relationship ended.

When she joined The Christian and Missionary Alliance, she was sent to join Eva in Hwodjou. Mildred was twenty-two and full of energy. Her laughter was so hearty that it convulsed her whole body. She delighted in riding out to the villages, where she visited the people and shared the gospel with them in their language.

At one point she regretfully left this open-air work to assume responsibility for a school to train women in Christian behavior. But eventually village work would become the primary way of life for Mildred and her partners.

## Francesca

Francesca was last to join the Trio. Born in 1871, she was Eva's younger sister. Although she was the quietest of the three, she could hold her own. She once debated with the witty Catholic journalist G.K. Chesterton, who joked that she ought to be burnt as a heretic for opposing him.

Francesca entered the mission field later than the other two because she had remained behind to care for her dying mother. Trained as a nurse, she was sensitive and sympathetic. If Eva was the skeptic and Mildred the enthusiast, Francesca was the calm, dependable, cautious one. The three worked as a harmonious team until their deaths.

## Gossiping the Gospel

In 1911 the Trio took a timely furlough just as the Republican revolution was heating up in China. When the women returned to Hwodjou after their furlough, it was with serious thoughts of moving on to undertake other work.

Courtesy Elisee Reclus, *The Earth and Its Inhabitants* (New York: D. Appleton, 1895)

*The Gobi Desert around 1895*

The Church leaders pleaded with the Trio to remain, but Eva felt that the Chinese Church would never mature if it remained dependent on European leadership. On June 11, 1923, the Trio headed for Gansu Province in Central Asia, carrying with them a cartload of Bibles and literature. "Our aim will be to visit every city of the Gansu Province located beyond the Great Wall," they wrote. Before they left, they heard that two women missionaries were in the hands of bandits. They went anyway.

Because they wanted to visit China's people in their markets and homes, as Mildred had done in her early days at Hwodjou, their journey was slow. They spoke with as many Chinese people as they could, turning every conversation to Christ and "gossiping the gospel."

They accepted danger and privation as a part of their journey. For example, they cooked over a fire fueled by camel dung, which they collected along the way. At one point soldiers tried to coerce them into paying for "protection," and when they refused to pay, they were cursed: "May your carts overturn, your baggage be stolen, and for your stinginess may you be robbed." Another time, the axle of their cart snapped in a mud hole and they had to wait a day for repairs. In Gansu Province, the first inn they slept in was a cave. Its walls were filthy and its floor littered with animal fodder. Men and women alike slept upon the *kang*, a heater that was usually smoky and smelly (because it was fueled with dung) but was unlit that cold night.

The Trio did not always eat well and therefore enjoyed a good meal all the more when they could get it. Once, at Hami, they were served rice with Shantow bread; chopped mutton with fried aubergines; French beans; sauteed, sliced cucumber; cantaloupe and tea made with sweet water. The last item was especially welcome after the brackish water holes of the desert.

## Answers to Prayer

The three women had been in Gansu for only a few days when Dr. Kao, a Chinese Christian who had moved to Gandjou so that he could act as a witness in that pagan city, sent them a letter pleading for their help. Years before, they had heard Dr. Kao speak. They decided to honor his invitation.

Their road was beautiful but hard. On the last day of the journey, they rose at 3:00 a.m. to be sure that they would reach Gandjou on time. While they were still many miles away, their cart sank to its axle and could not be extracted. Hungry and desperate, they ate cold dough fried in linseed oil. The oil made them gag.

When their situation was beginning to seem hopeless, a man on horseback appeared. It was Dr. Kao. He took charge of the situation, sent for extra horses and was able to pull them out. Eighteen hours after their early start, the Trio arrived in Gandjou, broken with fatigue.

Dr. Kao was a man of prayer, and the Gandjou Christians had begun praying with him several weeks earlier that the Lord would send experienced Christians to them. Dr. Kao and two or three local Christians had even gone into the Tibetan hills to spend time before God, asking for His guidance. Now, in answer to prayer, not just one but three missionaries had arrived.

*When the China Trio found a man dying of thirst in the Gobi Desert, their cart driver urged them to leave him, but they answered him, "Nothing will induce us to leave a dying man to his fate." They took turns walking so that he might ride in their cart, and the man recovered. Actions like this were typical of Eva, Mildred and Francesca.*

Dr. Kao made the Trio an offer: If they would stay and teach the Christians of Gandjou, the Christians would send a band of men and women with them to spread the gospel in the surrounding region. In fact, the novice Christians had already begun this work, but they were painfully aware that they needed a better grounding in Scripture in order to be effective. The Trio agreed to the arrangement.

## On the Edge of the Gobi

Thus began one of the most extraordinary gospel adventures in history. Five or six times over the next fifteen years, the three women visited every oasis town and village that lay outside the Great Wall in the province of Gansu. They sold books and gossiped the gospel. To and fro across the desert they journeyed, trekking on foot, riding camels or traveling by cart, visiting the bazaars and oases of Central Asia, meeting people of many races and tongues. At fairs they erected their great white tent and crammed it with eager listeners.

*Before we reached Dove Tower, the sun was high and the scorching heat almost intolerable. All the same on we jolted, sitting upon some mysterious boxes, which were the cargo of our new conveyance; but before long the aroma with which we seemed to be surrounded caused us to enquire what merchandise was being conveyed over this desert road. "Dead mules," was the answer. "Two of mine have just died, so I have packed them into these boxes to sell for meat further down the road." The end of the incident was that we bought the meat, and promptly abandoned it!*

*—from* Through Jade Gate

While selling the Scriptures, Eva learned to feign reluctance when opening her packages. To a Chinese person, this body language meant that she was holding back a real treasure. "Open that bundle and let me see what you have there!" they would say. She would hesitate, take up a copy of a gospel and say, "Why not take this one?" "No, that's only a portion. I want the whole thing," they would respond.

In temples, the three gospel-bearers spoke to priests about the true way to God and left Scriptures with them. Despite the opposition of rival faiths, the posters that they hung would be on the walls a year later when they returned.

They visited the Lake of the Crescent Moon, hidden so naturally by the desert that they could have passed a hundred feet on any side of it and never have seen it. It was there that Eva led them sliding down the dunes.

They visited the Courts of Hell, caves that depicted the torments of the damned. The entrance to the caves greeted pilgrims with the words "What? So you have come, too?"

At Sudjou they could find no suitable place to stay. They prayed, and a large property with fine rooms and a pavilion was offered to them. By means of posters hung around the city, they informed the people that they had come. A great celebration was about to begin, and the missionaries and their helpers prepared parcels of books and tracts, wrapping them in scarlet paper to lure buyers. Their team visited every shop in town, offering brightly flowered posters to the shopkeepers to brighten their drab walls. To prime conversations, the three women paused before homes where sewing was taking place and commented on the ladies' needlework. They opened a school, and those who came to gawk heard them sing and share the gospel. Some went away believing.

Everywhere they went they saw the terrible effects of opium and proclaimed that God could deliver people from the drug. They gave lessons in the phonetic alphabet that allowed Chinese people to learn to read in weeks instead of years. They treated diseases and astonished everyone by rescuing babies whom others had thrown away. They admired carved Buddhas and rare writings and whistled tunes so that they could watch sand lizards freeze, spellbound, unable to move.

## Following the Ancient Silk Road

Centuries ago, silk was transported from China to the West down the old silk road across the treacherous Gobi Desert, where travelers plodded in the cool night and rested during the hot day. Marco Polo had passed that way, and the women passed that way too, in 1926, as they were traveling home to England by way of the Soviet Union.

In 1929 they were back in Gansu, ready to begin their longest gospel journey ever. Rebellion broke out in the area, and for eight months the Trio were held by Muslim brigands near Tun hwang. One day a message came from General "Thunderbolt" Ma, the rebel warlord, that the women must appear before him. He was wounded and asked them a medical question. They treated him and his soldiers, and after many days they asked to be allowed to return to Tun hwang. Permission was granted.

Mildred bravely faced the twenty-one-year-old tyrant and urged him to take care of his soul. He just stared at her. The women left, but for the next eight months they were kept under the command of Ma's generals.

So, they planned an escape. They began by setting aside a portion of each day's rations and regularly riding out on short preaching trips. As long as they were home by nightfall, nothing was said. One day, however, they did not return. Instead, they kept going, fleeing toward the Sinkiang border with the rations they had saved.

Ma's authority extended for hundreds of miles, and more than once the Trio was challenged, but each time they were able to talk their way to safety. Finally, they reached a safe village and found shelter.

Later that day, when Mildred went out to care for the animals and did not return, the others looked for her and found her unconscious on the straw—she had been kicked by a mule. For several days she lay ill. As soon as she could travel, however, they pressed on, heading across the Gobi again to return to England for a much-needed rest in 1926.

## The Last Days of the Trio

One last time in 1928, the Trio returned to China, their adopted land, and settled again in Sudjou. But in 1936 all foreigners were ordered out of the city. Tired and feeling their age, the three admitted that their work in China was over. Mildred suffered continual insomnia and strain. They said their final farewells and returned to England, rejoicing that this time they were able to travel part of the way by air.

In England they settled into a little cottage and watched sadly as World War II began. Even in England they were unable to escape adventure. One day a German missile leveled their cottage. Eva was pulled from the wreckage and dusted off, having sustained only cuts and bruises; Francesca's head was hit by a door frame; Mildred had to walk out barefoot over broken glass. But, all three, as well as their secretary and an adopted girl, came out alive and not seriously injured.

The adventures of the dynamic Trio made them in great demand as speakers. Not just the Church, but geographic societies and travel organizations asked them to speak. For their achievements they were awarded the Livingstone Medal of the Royal Scottish Geographical Society, and Mildred was awarded the 1942 Lawrence Memorial Medal by the Royal Central Asian Society.

Over the years, Mildred and Francesca had recorded their adventures in books—twenty altogether. Queen Consort Elizabeth entertained the Trio at Buckingham Palace and sent copies of their book, *The Gobi Desert*, to people as Christmas presents.

Mildred was the first to die in 1952. Eva lived to be ninety, and during her last illness, Francesca slept on the floor beside Eva to care for her. Scolded for sleeping on the floor, Francesca replied, "I've been sleeping on floors all my life." She outlived her older sister by only three weeks.

*Recommended reading: W.J. Platt,* Three Women: Mildred Cable, Francesca French, Evangeline French *(London: Hodder and Stoughton, 1964).*

# SHE CHANGED HER MIND

*I*da Scudder wanted to leave hot, overcrowded India for the good life. If she had been asked to define "the good life," she would have replied, "Society, America, marriage to a millionaire."

She had been born in India, and her memories of her childhood there were ugly. Had she not been forced as a small girl to break bread to feed children who were too weak to feed themselves? Had she not seen their tiny corpses lying beside the road? India was not the place for her.

However, Ida's ambition changed in one single, terrible night in 1892. As she read in her room, a high-caste Brahmin stepped onto her veranda. He asked her to come attend to his child-wife, who was in labor. The barber women—India's midwives—had done all they could. Without help, the girl would die.

Ida replied that she knew nothing about midwifery. Her father, a skilled doctor, was not at home, but she would take him to the girl as soon as he returned. The Brahmin refused. "She had better die than have a man come into the house," he said.

Ida felt pity for the poor girl. But what could she do? She returned to her book.

Again there were footsteps on the veranda. Was the Brahmin back? Ida ran downstairs, where she found a Mohammedan. "Please," he pleaded. "Come help my wife." She was dying in labor.

Ida's father, John Scudder, was home by then, and he offered to go, but the Mohammedan refused. No man outside his family had ever looked on his wife's face. He could not let a foreign male approach her. Neither Ida nor John could change the man's mind. Ida returned to her room, but she could take no interest in her book.

## Ida Scudder

**Born:** December 9, 1870, in Ranipat, India
**Education:** Educated as a medical doctor
**Married:** Did not marry
**Children:** None
**Died:** 1959 in India
**Quote:** "Don't err on the side of being too small."

31

*O*fficials claimed that Ida's students could never compete with men in the medical exams. The tests were so hard that she'd be lucky to have a single woman pass. As the results of the exam were announced, the stress mounted. Only twenty percent of the men had passed! Then the women's scores were read. Inspired by Ida's vision, all of her students had passed.

*A third time she heard footsteps, and, to her horror, a third man appeared. He was a high-caste Hindu, and he too had a young wife who was dying in labor. He wanted to know if Ida would come, because only a woman could tend to his wife.*

*Later, Ida wrote:*

> *I could not sleep that night—it was too terrible. [Here] were three young girls dying because there was no woman to help them. I spent much of the night in anguish and prayer. I did not want to spend my life in India. My friends were begging me to return to the joyous opportunities of a young girl in America, and somehow I felt I could not give that up. I went to bed in the early morning after praying much for guidance. I think that was the first time I ever met God face to face, and all that time it seemed that He was calling me into this work.*

> *Early in the morning I heard the "tom-tom" beating in the village and it struck terror in my heart, for it was a death message. I sent our servant, who had come up early, to the village to find out the fate of these three women, and he came back saying that all of them had died during the night. . . . Again I shut myself in my room and thought very seriously about the condition of the Indian women and, after much thought and prayer, I went to my father and mother and told them that I must go home and study medicine, and come back to India to help such women.*

## "You Can Try"

Fortunately for Ida, women such as Elizabeth Blackwell had forged a passage for other women who wished to enter medical school. This meant that Ida would be able to study at top-notch schools. Her decision to become a medical missionary did not seem implausible to a public that was already aware of the work of Clara Swain, the first woman medical missionary.

When Ida returned to India in 1900, it was as a well-trained doctor. She also had in hand a substantial sum of money with which to build a women's hospital at Vellore. The money had come to her miraculously.

Mission leaders had asked Ida to raise the funds for building the hospital before she left. "But I sail for India in a week!" she had protested.

"We have a letter from Dr. Louisa Hart. She suggests you." The mission leaders waited for Ida's response.

Ida remembered the child brides, pregnant before their bodies were ripe for babies. She thought of sick women locked behind walls, forbidden to drink anything because the priests said it was dangerous. Yes, a women's hospital was needed. "We'll need $50,000 to build a good one," she replied.

Courtesy the Vellore Center

*Ida in a donated Peugeot, the first (and very noisy) car in Vellore*

"$50,000!" The men across from her gasped (it was a sum equivalent to at least $500,000 today), and in response they reduced the amount of money that Ida was allowed to solicit: "$8,000 is more realistic. We doubt you'll be able to raise even half that amount, but you can try."

Ida felt that the mission leaders were wrong. If the money was needed, God would provide it. However, a week was not much time. She threw herself at once into fundraising, calling on anyone she thought of who might be able to help her raise the sum. Dollars came in a trickle; it was "an ounce of water to quench an elephant's thirst," she said. Was the board right?

A friend mentioned to Ida that Miss Harriet Taber, president of a missionary society, lived nearby. Ida threw her shawl on at once and hurried to Harriet's home. There she poured out her heart, telling Harriet of India's need and her own call to the work. Harriet was interested. She arranged for Ida to speak to the women's society the following Monday.

On Sunday morning Ida received a note asking her to call on Mr. Schell, president of a New York bank, on Monday. Mr. Schell was an elderly brother-in-law of Harriet Taber. He had met Ida at his sister-in-law's house. A known tightwad, he might still be good for $500, so Ida readily paid the call.

Unknown to her, Mr. Schell had overheard her entire impassioned plea to Harriet. He grilled the young woman with questions about her proposed work. "And what

*August 13, 1935. A busy morning operating until twelve. Bible class in p.m. and then hurried to Medical Association, then to Ladies' Recreation Club, delightful dinner about 60 there.*

*August 14. Went to Gudiyattam. It's so wonderful having the little hospital there, with one of our own doctors in residence. Long and intensly interesting day. 478 patients with 77 lepers.*

*—Ida Scudder*

makes you think that you, a mere girl, can run a hospital?" he asked. Ida replied that she would be working beside her father, an experienced doctor. Satisfied, Mr. Schell turned and wrote a check. He requested that Ida name the hospital for his late wife, Mary Taber Schell.

When Ida saw the size of the check, she could hardly contain herself for delight. It was for $10,000! This evidence of God's power led her to reprove the board. "Now there, there would have been my $50,000 if you had not stopped me!" she exclaimed.

## "Oh, for the Quiet Order of a Well-Run Insane Asylum!"

India's need was overwhelming. There was one trained doctor for every 10,000 people. Traditional practitioners had a few excellent remedies, but they had even more that were harmful to their patients. For example, a "doctor" might treat an eye disease with a concoction of ground pepper and glass.

Ida's compassion revolted at this quackery. With no facilities to use (the Mary Taber Schell women's hospital could not be built for two years), she turned an eight-by-twelve room in her home into her dispensary. Her veranda served as a waiting room.

She didn't see any patients, however. Suspicion kept the Tamil Indians away. Her first call was to a desperate case for whom she could do nothing. Word spread that her patient had died, and the suspicion increased.

Eventually a high-caste Hindu came to Ida to have her eyes examined. She had a dangerous case of conjunctivitis, and Ida treated it successfully. Demands for her services increased steadily after that. Soon she was seeing so many cases that she had to conscript her willing kitchen maid to help her. Salomi was the first of many nurses Ida would train.

Compassion drove Ida to take on more and more work, and soon she and her nurses were seeing 100, 200, 300 and even 500 cases a day. Sometimes she exclaimed, "Oh, for the quiet order of a well-run insane asylum!"

## *Women Caring for Women*

Even if dozens more doctors had come from America and Europe, their services would have been like a drop of water in an ocean. Ida knew that Indian women needed to be taught to care for each other. That led Ida to create a nursing school in Vellore. Her first seven nurses graduated in 1905. But, as soon as the school opened, Ida set her sights higher. If she could train nurses, then she could train doctors as well. By 1922 she had seen her first class of home-trained doctors graduate.

Vellore officially became a medical college in 1928. It did not come easily. Ida did the work of six people. Prominent feminist backers from America such as Gertrude Dodd, Hilda Olsen and Lucy Peabody struggled long and hard during the Great Depression and World War II to raise funds to support Vellore as it grew. Time after time the Lord allowed the work to come to the very brink of extinction before rescuing it.

At one crisis, Ida wrote:

> First ponder, then dare. Know your facts. Count the cost. Money is not the most important thing. What you are building is not a medical school. It is the kingdom of God. Don't err on the side of being too small. If this is the will of God that we should keep the college open, it has to be done.

And it *was* done. Thus it came about that the woman who had wanted to shake the dust of India from her feet became dear to the Indians' hearts. Some Indians knelt before Ida, believing her to be the incarnation of a god. She constantly had to shift her feet to escape the unwelcome worship. She won international fame, British and Indian officials presented her with high awards and Gandhi visited her.

Late in her life, Ida acquired a mansion that she had always dreamed of owning— she had even prayed for it—when it was auctioned to her for a small sum. She retired there, gardening and sometimes visiting Vellore. She died in 1959 after spending the day holding patients' hands and quieting babies while doctors treated them. Vellore still operates to this day, a testimony to her vision and faith.

*Recommended reading: Dorothy Clarke Wilson,* Dr. Ida: The Story of Dr. Ida Scudder of Vellore *(New York: McGraw-Hill, 1959).*

# Part 2
## More Than Homemakers

*Homemaking was
just part of their
accomplishments.*

# HE COULDN'T OUTRUN HER PRAYERS

Courtesy John Lord, *Beacon Lights of History* (New York: James Clarke, 1886)

*W*hen she was a teenager, Monica liked her wine, and she drank it often and in abundance. One day a servant girl taunted Monica, calling her a drunkard. The servant's words cut deep, causing Monica to realize how wrong it was for her, as a Christian, to be living the way she was. She stopped drinking after that day and cleaned up her life. She went on to become one of the most famous mothers in Church history.

## Monica

**Born:** Around 331 in North Africa

**Education:** Taught by a Christian slave at home

**Married:** Patricius, a pagan, sometime before 354

**Children:** At least three

**Died:** 387 in North Africa

**Quote:** "All I wished to live for was that I might see you . . . a child of heaven."

## A Mother's Quiet Perseverance

Most of what we know about Monica comes from the writings of her son, Augustine, one of the most influential Christians of all time. She was born into a moderately wealthy family around AD 331 in North Africa. An old Christian maidservant, who had also cared for Monica's father when he was a baby, imparted her Christian faith to Monica and brought her up in it.

Monica was given in marriage to Patricius, who was not a Christian. For many years Monica sought to win him to the Lord, acting on the advice of First Peter 3:1-6, which tells women to be submissive, chaste and respectful and to dress simply. Monica realized that her conduct more than her words would be the means of Patricius' conversion. Quiet behavior was not easy, however, because Patricius easily lost his temper and, what is more, cheated on her continuously. But,

*Augustine consid-ered Monica the driving force behind his conversion. In his* **Confes-sions,** *he documented her relentless prayers and persuasion:*

> *My mother, your faithful servant, was weeping for me to you, weeping more than mothers weep for the bodily deaths of their sons. For she, by that faith and spirit, which she had from you, saw the death in which I lay and you, Lord, heard her prayer. You heard her and did not despise her tears which fell streaming and watered the ground beneath her eyes in every place where she prayed; and indeed you heard her.*

> *—Augustine (translated by Rex Warner)*

Monica's strategy prevailed. By persevering in patience and meekness, she won her mother-in-law to Christ and Patricius himself eventually became a Christian, though only toward the end of his life.

Monica's Christianity was not lived out just in the home. She was often a peacemaker between others who were at odds. In healing disputes, she never repeated the evil, bitter or hateful words that one side might express against the other. She also sought to help and minister to those who were teachers or pastors in the Church.

## Her Struggle to Win Her Family

Monica prayed that her family might eventually all come to Christ. She attempted to bring her children up in the ways of the Lord, and it pained her to see them stray from the truth she had taught them.

Her most promising son, Augustine, was given an excellent education, and Monica hoped that it might be a means for him to more fully reach God. Augustine, however, ignored his mother's warnings against youthful lusts and pursued a life of self-gratification and immorality while continuing his classical education. He lived with a woman who was not his wife and fathered a child. Monica didn't have the words to convince her son of the truth of Christianity, but she determined never to stop praying that he would turn to God.

## A Widow in Italy

Augustine tried to shake his mother off and by trickery left her behind in Carthage while he fled to Italy. Some time afterward, Monica, who was widowed, followed him. In Milan she attended the church that was pastored by the learned bishop Ambrose and rejoiced when Ambrose befriended Augustine. He was a man who could give her son intelligent answers to his questions about Christianity. Under Ambrose's preaching, Augustine eventually did move toward Christianity and experienced a powerful conversion.

Monica died in 387 at the age of fifty-six. In his *Confessions* Augustine spoke of his grief and of weeping for the mother "now gone from my sight, who for years had wept over me, that I might live in [God's] sight." Monica died a happy woman, for she had seen her prayers answered as both her husband and her son became believers.

Augustine was only thirty-three at the time of his mother's death, and many years of service to Christ and the Church lay before him. In later years he looked back on his life and recognized the importance of his mother's perseverance in prayer to his salvation and subsequent ministry. Neither Augustine nor Monica could have foreseen that Augustine's ministry would remain influential for centuries after his death and show itself in the thinking of men such as Luther, Calvin and countless other theologians from various traditions for the reforming, purifying and strengthening of the Church.

Courtesy Henry W. Ruoff, *Masters of Achievement* (Buffalo, NY: Frontier Press, 1910)

*Augustine as Bishop of Hippo*

*Recommended reading: Augustine of Hippo,* Confessions *(available from many publishers).*

# SETTING
## *the*
# PATTERN

*C*atherine von Bora was born in Lippendorf, Germany, *a few years before the Reformation burst into full flower. She was only eighteen when Martin Luther issued his now-famous ninety-five theses at Wittenburg in 1517. She had lived in the cloister of Marienthron, away from her father and three brothers, since she was three, having been taken there by her father after her mother's death. (He planned to remarry and did not want to impose the responsibility of caring for Catherine on his new wife.)*

*Upon hearing Luther's biblical teaching, Katie and several of the other nuns at the cloister wanted to leave their captivity in the convent. When Luther heard of this, he encouraged a merchant friend to help them escape. Merchant Kopp often delivered herring to the convent, and one evening in 1523, he bundled twelve nuns into his wagon in the empty fish barrels. Several of the nuns returned to their families; Luther helped find homes, husbands or positions for the rest.*

*Within two years after their fish-barrel ride, all of the nuns had been provided for except one—Katie. Gradually, through the persuasion of friends and his father— and through Katie's own bold offer—Luther proposed to marry her himself.*

## Katie Luther

**Born:** January 29, 1499, in Lippendorf, Germany
**Education:** Took classes at the Cloister of Marienthron
**Married:** Martin Luther on June 13, 1525
**Children:** Six
**Died:** December 20, 1552
**Quote:** *"I will stick to Christ as a burr to a topcoat."*

## Bringing Order to Luther's Life

Luther had been given the Augustinian monastery at Wittenburg, and it was into this monastery that Katie moved after her marriage to Luther in

*L*uther was ill and thought he was dying. He urged Katie to accept God's will, and she replied:

My dear Doctor [she always called him "Doctor" out of respect], if it is God's will I would rather have you with our Lord than here. But I am not thinking just of myself and Hans. There are so many people that need you. But don't worry about us. God will take care of us.

1525. She cleaned up the monastery and brought some order to Luther's daily life. Luther wrote to a friend, "There is a lot to get used to in the first year of marriage. One wakes up in the morning and finds a pair of pigtails on the pillow which were not there before."

After a year of marriage, Luther wrote to another friend, "My Katie is in all things so obliging and pleasing to me that I would not exchange my poverty for the riches of Croesus." Luther, the formerly celibate monk, now exalted marriage, exclaiming, "There is no bond on earth so sweet, nor any separation so bitter, as that which occurs in a good marriage."

Katie managed the finances of the family and helped to free Luther's mind for writing, teaching and ministering. Luther called her the "morning star of Wittenberg" since she rose at 4:00 a.m. to care for her many responsibilities. She tended the vegetable garden, the orchard, the fish pond and the barnyard animals, even going so far as to butcher them herself.

Often there were as many as thirty students, guests or boarders staying in the monastery, all of whom came under Katie's care. Also, Luther was often ill, and Katie was able to minister to him in his illnesses because of her mastery of herbs, poultices and massage.

Katie's life was not just concerned with the physical, however. Luther encouraged Katie in her Bible study and suggested particular passages for her to memorize.

## A Model Family

In time the Luthers had six children and also raised four orphans. Luther viewed marriage as a school for character. He said that family life helped train Christians in the virtues of fortitude, patience, charity and humility. For centuries the reformer's family served as a model for German families.

After Luther's death in 1546, Katie lived for six more years—long enough to see all her children (except Magdalena, who had died young) achieve positions of influence.

As the wife of Martin Luther, Katie was always in the public eye. Had she not handled that position as well as she did, Luther's ministry would have suffered embarrassment as he stood against a celibate clergy and endorsed marriage. Because of Luther's prominence, other wives took their cues from Katie. It is a tribute to her godly character that she took on such a heavy responsibility, was so gracious to those in need and managed her household so well, demonstrating to a watching world what thrift and hard work could accomplish.

Courtesy Arthur Cushman McGiffert, *Martin Luther* (New York: Century, 1911)

*The Luther home, which was formerly a monastery*

*Recommended reading: William J. Peterson,* Martin Luther Had a Wife *(Wheaton, IL: Tyndale, 1983).*

# PURITAN WIFE *and* MOTHER

Depiction of a pilgrim woman. Courtesy Frank Moody Gregg, *The Founding of a Nation* (Cleveland: Arthur H. Clark, 1915)

*A nne Bradstreet probably never expected to see her po-
ems in print. As a matter of fact, they were published
only as a result of a bit of skulduggery. Her brother-in-law, John
Woodbridge, secretly made copies of her writing and took them to England, where he published them without her knowledge or permission. The world has been grateful ever since.*

## Sailing to a New Land

### Anne Bradstreet

**Born:** Around 1612 in North-
ampton, England
**Education:** Privately tu-
tored
**Married:** Simon Bradstreet
in 1628
**Children:** Eight
**Died:** September 16, 1672,
in Andover, MA
**Quote:** "Upon the rock
Christ Jesus will I build
my faith."

In recent history the Puritans have often been characterized as sour-faced, dull, never-smiling haters of fun and happiness. However, this distorted impression does not reflect the vibrant lives that most Puritans lived. Take, for example, Anne Bradstreet, a model Puritan woman whose soaring spirit, zest for life, intense love for her husband and children and beautiful poetry refute the stereotype.

There is no clear record of the date of Anne's birth, but it is believed to have been sometime in 1612 in Northampton, England. At age eighteen, Anne was among the hundreds of English Puritans who sailed for America under the leadership of John Winthrop in 1630. Also taking part in this migration were Thomas and Dorothy Dudley, Anne's parents, and her husband, Simon Bradstreet.

In England, Thomas Dudley had been steward to the Earl of Lincoln, and Anne and her family had enjoyed the advantages of wealth. She was fond of

*In 1650 Master Ste-
phen Bowtell, a Lon-
don publisher and book-
seller, published a book of
poems titled* THE TENTH
MUSE Lately Sprung up in
AMERICA, OR Severall Po-
ems. *The book marked a
milestone in English and
American literature. It contained the first verses by
an American that could
stand beside England's poetry, and more than that,
it was the first volume of
enduring English-language
poetry produced by a wo-
man. The author was Anne
Bradstreet.*

learning, and when she was about seven, several tu-
tors were hired to teach her dancing, music and languages, among other subjects. In 1628, when she
was sixteen, she married Simon Bradstreet, the son
of a Puritan minister and himself a member of the
Earl of Lincoln's household.

Although the young couple could anticipate a
comfortable life materially, they chose to leave much
of their wealth in England and move to America
where they could worship God in the way they preferred and with greater freedom.

Anne's household would be an influential one
in the new land. Both her father and Simon were
active in the governmental affairs of Massachusetts Bay Colony, and each served several terms as
governor of the colony.

## Anne the Poet

In the midst of her household duties, Anne found
time to write poetry. Evidently, some of her contemporaries criticized her for this, saying that writing
was not an appropriate activity for a woman. We
find evidence of this tension in her poem "The Pro-
logue": "I am obnoxious to each carping tongue/
Who says my hand a needle better fits."

In spite of the criticism, Anne wrote on. Several of her poems were written to her husband, expressing how much she missed him while he was absent on government business. The simplest of these poems beautifully told of her love:

> If ever two were one, then surely we.
> If ever man were lov'd by wife, then thee;
> If ever wife was happy in a man,
>
> Compare with me ye women if ye can.
> I prize thy love more than whole Mines of gold,
> Or all the riches that the East doth hold.

At the beginning of her marriage, Anne feared that she might have no children, but the
Lord heard her prayers, and she and Simon eventually had eight. Many of her poems were

written as prayers in the midst of the events of her active family's life. Such was the poem "Upon My Daughter Hannah Her Recovery from a Dangerous Fever":

> Blest be thy Name who did'st restore
> To health my Daughter dear
> When death did seem ev'n to approach
> And life was ended near.
> Grant she remember what thou'st done
> And celebrate thy praise
> And let her Conversation say
> She loves thee all her Days.

Courtesy Anne Bradstreet, edited by John Harvard Ellis, *The Words of Anne Bradstreet, 1867*

### Simon Bradstreet

Many of Anne's poems were written during times of hardship or tragedy. Her poetry was her means to again focus on her God and His matchless plan and love for her. This can be seen in "Verses upon the Burning of Our House, July 10th, 1666":

> Thou hast an house on high erect,
> Fram'd by that mighty Architect,
> With glory richly furnished,
> Stands permanent though this be fled.
> It's purchased, and paid for too
> By him who hath enough to do.
> A Price so vast as is unknown,
> Yet, by his Gift, is made thine own.
> There's wealth enough, I need no more;
> Farewell my Self, farewell my Store.
> The world no longer let me Love,
> My hope and Treasure lies Above.

Another poem, written about her longing for Simon, exhibits her usual religious theme, quaint spelling and clear meaning: "Lord, bee thou Pilott to the ship, / And send them prosperous gailes; / In storms and sickness, Lord, preserve. / Thy goodness never failes."

A volume of Anne's poetry, *The Tenth Muse*, was published by her brother-in-law without her knowledge in 1650. The poems in that volume were not as lively as the family poems that are quoted in this chapter and which appeared in later editions of Anne's poetry. Most of the pieces in *The Tenth Muse* were lengthy, poetic treatments of learned subjects, such as the epochs of history, the four monarchies of Daniel (Babylon, Persia, Greece and

> *A*mong all my ex-
> periences of God's
> gracious dealings with me,
> I have constantly observ-
> ed this—that he has never
> suffered me long to sit
> loose from him, but by
> one affliction or other has
> made me look home and
> search what was amiss.
> —Anne Bradstreet

Rome) and the seasons. They are scholarly poems written in a style that would be expected more from a poet in a European court than from a woman on the American frontier. The book was well received in both America and England. A century later, John Newton (author of "Amazing Grace") highly praised Anne's work.

## Overcoming Hardships and Doubt

Going to the American wilderness to settle was a venture filled with hardships, and Anne suffered repeated illnesses throughout her forty years in America. She recognized, however, that life is filled with testings and that hardships bring a greater reliance on the Lord. She thanked her God for bringing her closer to Him through her ailments.

In an age filled with religious controversies and wars, Anne also faced doubt and uncertainty, but she cast her hope on Christ.

> There is but one Christ, who is the Sun of righteousness, in the midst of an innumerable company of Saints and Angels; those Saintes have their degrees even in this life, some are stars of the first magnitude, and some of lesse degree; and others (and indeed the most in number), but small and obscure, yet all receive their luster (be it more or less) from that glorious sun that inlightens all in all.

Shortly before her death by consumption in 1672, Anne concluded an account of her spiritual pilgrimage that she had written for her children. Part of it reads as follows:

> Upon this Rock Christ Jesus will I build by faith, and if I perish, I perish, But I know all the powers of Hell shall never prevail against it, I know whom I have trusted, and whom I have believed and that he is able to keep what I have committed to his charge.

*Recommended reading: Elizabeth Wade White,* **Anne Bradstreet: The Tenth Muse** *(New York: Oxford University Press, 1971).*

# Oh, Susannah!

Courtesy Warren Dunham Foster, *Heroines of Modern Religion* (New York: Sturgis and Walton, 1913)

*W*hen Susannah Annesley, the twenty-fifth child of Dr. Samuel Annesley, was born to his second wife in 1669, there probably was not much discussion about her or her future. Little could the family dream that she would become the mother of John and Charles Wesley, the founders of worldwide Methodism.

Susannah was an "old lady of nineteen" when she became the wife of Samuel Wesley, an Anglican minister, in 1688. The Wesley family traced their lineage back to the tenth century, but ancestry did little to ease the problems Susannah and Samuel faced in their forty-four years of marriage. They suffered illness, disease, poverty and the deaths of children. Fire twice destroyed their home. But, through it all, Susannah accepted the will of God and placed herself and her family in His hands.

## Susannah Wesley

**Born:** January 20, 1669, in London, England

**Education:** Well-educated; no details known

**Married:** Samuel Wesley on November 11, 1688

**Children:** Nineteen

**Died:** July 23, 1742

**Quote:** "I will tell you what rule I observed when I was young, and too much addicted to childish diversions: Never to spend more time in mere recreation in one day than I spent in private religious devotions."

## Differences of Opinion

Politically, Samuel and Susannah were both members of the Tory party (a political group), but while Samuel accepted William of Orange as King William III, Susannah considered James II to be the true king. Once, in 1701, Susannah refused to say "Amen" to Samuel's prayer for King William. Tension ensued, and Samuel left for

*Susannah Wesley bore as many as nineteen children. Only half of them grew to adulthood, but with each of them she spent an hour every week in a quiet heart-to-heart talk, directing them to God. John's hour was on Thursday. So sacred did that special time remain in his memory that afterward when he had left home, he asked his mother to spend it in prayer for him.*

London as a convocation proctor for a year. He returned in 1702 when Queen Anne, whom they both acknowledged as the legitimate sovereign, came to the throne. So, in a real sense we might say that John, who was born in 1703, was the child of their reconciliation.

## Methodical Manager of Her Home

Susannah bore between seventeen and nineteen children; ten survived into adulthood. The frequent absences of her husband while he was on church business left the management of the household in her hands. At those times, she led the family prayers, which were ordinarily Samuel's responsibility, and she did so with such grace that neighbors asked to be included. She imparted to others her steadfast faith not only through the Scriptures but through her own example of daily trust in God.

Susannah raised her children strictly. John's future methodical nature may have been impressed upon him by his mother. Her children were taught to cry softly, to eat what was put before them and not to raise their voices or play noisily. No wish was granted to a child who whined or cried. Physical punishment was used, but confession of faults could sometimes avert it. Susannah also made her children speak politely to the servants. All but one of the children learned to read by the age of five, including the girls.

After a 1709 fire in which their home was almost destroyed by arson, the family discipline broke down, but Susannah managed to restore order. She paid special attention to John, who was almost lost in that fire. Only by forming a human ladder were the neighbors able to save the lad as he stood crying at the attic window. He later referred to himself as "a brand plucked from the burning fire," and his mother said that she intended to be more particularly careful of the soul of this child that "Thou hast so mercifully provided for, than ever I have been, that I may do my endeavours to instill into his mind the disciplines of Thy true religion and virtue."

## Never Such a Woman

It is said that at the age of six or seven, John thought he would never marry "because I could never find such a woman as my father had." After Samuel Wesley died in 1735, Susannah lived with her children, especially John, with whom she spent most of her last year. She died on July 23, 1742, and was buried in London's Bunhill Fields, where John Bunyan and Isaac Watts are also buried. Her sons went on to win tens of thousands of souls to Christ. Susannah could not have wished for more.

Courtesy Herbert Asbury, *Methodist Saint* (New York: Knopf, 1927)

*A sketch of the Wesley home when it was on fire*

*Recommended reading: Kathy McReynolds,* Susanna Wesley: The Godly Mother of Two of Christianity's Most Gifted Men— John and Charles Wesley *(Minneapolis: Bethany House, 1998).*

# Part 3
## The Ultimate Price

*To them, life was
not more dear
than Christ.*

# IN *the* ARENA

Courtesy Thomas Armitage, *A History of the Baptists* (New York: Bryan, Taylor and Co., 1893)

*T*he bloodthirsty mob in the amphitheater had never seen such courage. Onlookers were astonished at the slave girl's victorious cry even in the midst of her pain and suffering: "I am a Christian and there is nothing vile done by us." Even though the crowd detested the Christians, they had to admit that never had a woman endured so many terrible tortures with such strength.

The year was 177 and the city was Lyons, Gaul (modern France). Christianity had first arrived in the city over twenty-five years earlier when Polycarp of Smyrna (in modern Turkey) sent Pothinus as a missionary to Gaul. Pothinus diligently established the Church of Christ in Lyons and nearby Viennes.

As the Church grew, spiritual resistance began to mount, and persecution against the Christians began. They were shut out of businesses and houses. They endured all kinds of indignities that were intended to shame them. Mobs formed to beat, stone and rob them. But when believers were arrested and examined by the city authorities, they boldly confessed their allegiance to Christ, and they were imprisoned to await the arrival of the governor to the region.

Some nonbelieving servants of the Christians were seized and threatened with torture if they did not testify against their masters. They devised all sorts of false accusations against the Christians, such as that they practiced cannibalism, incest and other shameful behaviors. These allegations enraged the mob even more.

## Blandina

**Born:** Unknown
**Education:** Unknown
**Married:** Not known to have married
**Children:** None
**Died:** 177 in Lyons, France
**Quote:** "I am a Christian and there is nothing vile done by us."

## Cruel Holiday Entertainment

August 1 was a holiday set aside to celebrate the greatness of Rome and its emperor. The governor

57

> *Blandina was filled with such power that those who by turns kept torturing her in every way from dawn until evening were worn out and exhausted, and themselves confessed defeat from lack of aught else to do to her; they marvelled that the breath still remained in a body all mangled and covered with gaping wounds, and they testified that a single form of torture was sufficient to render life extinct, let alone such and so many.*
>
> *—Blandina's church*

would be visiting on that day and was expected to show his patriotism by sponsoring entertainment for the whole city of Lyons. He considered his finances and decided that, since it was expensive to hire true gladiators, boxers and wrestlers, he would instead torture the imprisoned Christians as part of the holiday entertainment. That would cost him a good deal less and please the crowd every bit as much.

The Christians were confined in the darkest and most unhealthy part of the prison. The air was so bad that many of them suffocated there before they could even be brought to the amphitheater.

In an attempt to force confessions, some Christians were placed on the "hot seat." This was literally a human barbecue where the victim was chained onto a grate over burning coals. It seemed impossible that anyone could live and retain his sanity after being so cruelly tortured, yet the Christians not only persevered but exhorted and encouraged each other in their faith.

Pothinus, the ninety-two-year-old bishop of Lyons, died in his prison cell two days after his torture. His cell, which can be visited at the archaeological museum in Lyons, was about the size of a home electric dishwasher—so cramped that he could not have even stood upright.

Sanctus, a deacon from Viennes, stood firm in his faith even after red-hot plates were fastened to the most tender parts of his body and he was covered in wounds and bruises. He was "an example for the others, showing that nothing is fearful where the love of the Father is, and nothing is painful where there is the glory of Christ."

A slave girl named Blandina, about whose birth and early life we know nothing, was brought to witness these tortures and pressed to deny her faith and swear by idols so that she could escape similar punishment. She would not, and she was eventually subjected to the same horrors.

After enduring torture, some of the Christians were taken to the amphitheater where wild beasts devoured them to "entertain" the crowd. Among that group was the slave girl Blandina. She had already endured every imaginable torture and cruelty. She was suspended on a stake and exposed to the wild beasts. Because she appeared to be hanging on a cross and because of her intense prayers, she inspired the other Christians. When they looked at her, they were reminded of Christ who was crucified for them and of the Bible's promises that everyone who suffered for the glory of Christ would enjoy eternal fellowship with the living God. None of the beasts touched Blandina at the time, and she was taken down from the stake and cast back into prison. The Christians believed that God had preserved her for other contests so her victory over the evil spiritual forces might be even greater.

Courtesy Gateway Films

*The gate, only four feet high, to the tiny Roman cell in Lyons where Pothinus was held*

## Her Body Would Not Die

On the last day of the spectacle in the amphitheater, Blandina was brought in again with Ponticus, a boy of about fifteen. Amazingly, Blandina was still living after all she had been through. Ponticus died rather quickly, but Blandina held on to the last. She encouraged many others and saw them go on before her to Jesus. Finally, she was ready to hasten after them. She faced her death rejoicing—as if being called to a marriage feast rather than to wild beasts.

She was tortured from morning until night with every ingenuity that her tormenters could devise, but her body would not die. The report stated:

> After the scourging, after the wild beasts, after the roasting seat, she was finally enclosed in a net, and thrown before a bull. And having been tossed about by the animal, but feeling none of the things which were happening to her, on account of her hope and firm hold upon what had been entrusted to her, and her communion with Christ, she also was sacrificed.

Blandina and her fellow martyrs are memorialized by a marker that can be visited to-day at the place of their martyrdom in the ancient amphitheater at Lyons.

*Recommended reading: "The Martyrs of Lyon," http://www.gospelcom.net/chi/earlychurch/lyons.shtml.*

# EMBRACING
## *the*
# CROSS

Courtesy Maria Amata Neyer, *Edith Stein* (Washington, DC: ICS Publications, 1999). Used by permission.

*E*dith Stein hesitated outside the door. She had lost a good friend in Adolf, but Anna Reinach had lost more. How do you comfort a woman whose dearly loved husband has just been killed in war?

Edith entered the room, and to her surprise, she found Anna at peace. Instead of seeking comfort, Anna was comforting others.

## Edith Stein

**Born:** October 12, 1891, at Breslau

**Education:** Attended the universities of Breslau and Güttingen

**Married:** Did not marry

**Children:** None

**Died:** August 9, 1945, at Auschwitz

**Quote:** "One can only learn the 'Science of the Cross' if one feels the cross in one's own person."

Adolf Reinach had become a Christian while fighting at the front of the German battle lines in World War I. Following his lead, Anna too became a Christian, and they were both baptized as Lutherans. Now the widow was confident that, because of God's love, death had meaning.

Searching Anna's eyes, Edith knew that her friend had experienced a genuine change. "For the first time, I was seeing with my very eyes the church, born from its redeemer's sufferings, triumphant over the sting of death. That was the moment my unbelief collapsed and Christ shone forth—in the mystery of the cross."

Edith's conversion was still five years away, however. She was a Jew with a good deal of atheism, family opposition and philosophical baggage to overcome.

## From Tantrums to Atheism

Four of Edith's brothers and sisters died before she was even born; she was the eleventh and last child in a family of devout Jews. Curiously enough,

*The intellectual knows that supreme and ultimate truths do not manifest themselves through the workings of the human reason, and that when it comes to the most essential matters—those affecting the ordering of one's practical existence—it is possible for a higher degree of divine illumination to make a plain, uneducated person wiser than the most learned scholar.*

*At the same time, the intellectual recognizes that the natural functioning of the human reason does have a legitimate domain, and this is where he applies his efforts. He is like a farmer tilling his fields: he knows what he does is both good and useful, and yet within certain limits, as is all human endeavor.*

*—Edith Stein*

she was born on the most solemn Jewish holiday, the Day of Atonement, on October 12, 1891. "My mother laid great emphasis on the occurrence, and I think more than anything else, it made her youngest child especially dear to her," wrote Edith.

Edith hardly knew her father, because he died before she was two years old. After his death her mother had to manage the family lumber business, so Edith was virtually raised by an older sister. But, Mrs. Stein made it a point to come to the bedroom as soon as she got home from work to kiss Edith good night.

Despite the influence of her mother's love, Edith was subject to frightful temper tantrums when she didn't get her way. If anyone tried to move her during one of the tantrums, she became rigid. If she was locked up in her room, she pounded ceaselessly on her door to make everyone within hearing as miserable as she was.

Despite the tantrums, Edith was the "smart one" in the family. She was only four years old when her oldest brother carried her around the room, singing student songs to her, showing her pictures in a history of literature and telling her about the poets Schiller and Goethe. She forgot none of it. At age six, she demanded to bypass kindergarten and enter first grade. She even offered to give up her birthday presents in exchange. Admitted at midterm, she soon leapfrogged past the other children, despite their head start. "I could almost say I felt more at home there than in my own house," she wrote. Seeing how silly others looked when they were angry, she became ashamed of her tantrums, and they ceased. When she was seven, she became introspective and began living in an imaginary world in her head.

At thirteen, Edith became an atheist, but she did not announce it, not wanting to hurt her mother. She lost interest in school, and Mrs. Stein thought she was sick, so she sent Edith to stay with Else, an older sister. Eight months later, Edith returned to school, determined to become a teacher. She made friends, studied hard, played games—and searched for a reason to live now that she no longer believed in a personal God. In 1911, at age twenty, she passed her secondary school exams, but "instead of the great sense of happiness that I had expected, there was only a great inward emptiness."

## Soul Unmeasured, Spirit Unweighed

Edith entered the University of Breslau in March 1911. She was one of only a few women who did so. Longing for insight into the mysteries of the human experience and the soul, she enrolled in a psychology course. To her disappointment, she found that her teachers were interested only in things that could be measured and quantified—that is, converted into numbers. Since spirit cannot be seen or measured, they smiled skeptically when it was mentioned.

Certain that there must be more to human beings than chemical reactions, electrical impulses and genes, Edith searched for answers in the writings of others. She discovered Edmund Husserl's difficult book, *Logical Investigations*. Husserl had invented a philosophy known as phenomenology. He considered mental and spiritual events to be real phenomena that should be studied, and he criticized the kind of psychology that cared only about quantification. Husserl argued that many things may be understood only by intuition. His views were just what Edith was looking for.

## A Whole New World

Edith transferred to the University of Güttingen in 1913 so that she could study under Husserl. She was nervous about meeting "the master," but when they met, he quickly broke the ice. She informed him that she had read the entire second volume of *Logical Investigations*. "The entire second volume?" exclaimed Husserl. "Now, that I call heroic!" He took her on as his first assistant, and she edited his works. She wrote articles of her own, trying to understand the nature of spirit.

At Güttingen, Edith became intimate with a group of students who hiked, argued, danced and put on skits together. She also got to know Adolf Reinach and Max Schlerer. Schlerer, a convert to Christianity from Judaism, argued persuasively that religion alone makes a human being human. He identified humility as the prerequisite of all moral endeavor and said that its sole purpose was to bring one to lose himself in God, which would result in resurrection. Edith found this thought rich and fascinating and

Courtesy Maria Amata Neyer, *Edith Stein* (Washington, DC: ICS Publications, 1999). Used by permission.

*Edmund Husserl*

more helpful than Husserl's. "It was my first contact with a world that until then had been completely unfamiliar. I can't say that it led me directly to faith. But it did open up a whole new world of 'phenomena' that I wouldn't be able to pass by blindly anymore."

With the coming of World War I, Edith took time out of her studies to nurse wounded soldiers. When she returned to school a few months later in 1914, she began her doctoral thesis. She studied how people are able to empathize—to put themselves in others' shoes, as it were—and, more important, how they establish community with others, the kind of communion in which each can almost read the other's mind. Although she was still an atheist, unable to pray, she was genuinely seeking truth. Later she said that anyone who does that is actually seeking God, who is the truth. She was just twenty-five when she earned her doctorate, graduating *summa cum laude* in March 1917.

## References to Christ

After Adolph's death, Anna Reinach had asked Edith to organize his academic papers. In them, Edith found many references to Christ, and to understand them, she read through the New Testament for the first time. She came to believe that Christ is divine and knew that she wanted to become a Christian. But she was undecided: Should she become a Protestant or a Catholic? Many of her friends had become Protestants, so Edith read Kierkegaard's *Training in Christianity*, but she was turned off by his emphasis on a "leap of faith." But, when staying with a friend and looking for a book to read, she opened the autobiography of the fiery Spanish saint Teresa of Avila and could not close it until dawn. "This is truth," exclaimed Edith. As soon as the stores opened, she went out and bought a Catholic catechism and missal. On the first day of 1922 she was baptized.

Edith accepted a position teaching children at a Dominican school in Speyer. There she exchanged ideas with a Jesuit priest, and he convinced her that she could best serve God by continuing her scholarly search for truth. She translated Catholic classics into German, including St. Thomas Aquinas' *On Truth*, to which she added her own commentary. Her synthesis of phenomenology and Thomism marked her as an original mind. Her writings became popular, and she was asked to lecture. She also spoke out for feminist causes.

With little free time for prayer because of her teaching, lecturing, translating and charities, Edith spent whole nights on her knees in the school chapel.

## In the Name of All Jews

Edith found it difficult to obtain an academic position because she was both a woman and a Jew. She accepted a lectureship at the German Institute for Scientific Pedagogy in Munster in 1932, but was fired because of her race when the Nazis gained power. Ironically, Hitler's henchmen were firing her because of her Jewishness, while her mother considered her a traitor to her race for becoming a Christian.

Courtesy Maria Amata Neyer, *Edith Stein* (Washington, DC: ICS Publications, 1999). Used by permission.

*Edith and a sister*

When Edith had become a Christian, her mother had cried. It was the first time Edith had ever seen her shed tears, and that hurt Edith more than if she had been expelled from the family. She tried to explain that as a Christian she was moving deeper to the core of the Jewish faith, but her mother never understood.

In 1933 Edith became a Carmelite nun. She took as her new name Teresa Benedicta a Cruce, "Teresa, Blessed by the Cross." Her family suspected that her entrance into the convent was an attempt to escape anti-Semitism. This was not so. In fact, Edith was offered an opportunity to teach in South America but declined it because she believed that for the sake of the Jews, she must remain in Germany. "I spoke to our Savior and told Him that I knew it was His cross that was now being laid on the Jewish people. Most of them did not understand it; but those who did must accept it willingly in the name of all." After she spent thirteen hours in prayer, she rose, determined to intercede for the persecutors of the Jews.

Chief of those persecutors was Hitler. Under his regime, anti-Semitic literature and actions had become intolerable. Edith felt that she could bridge the gap of understanding between Jews and Christians by showing that people of the two faiths had similar experiences in their daily lives. During her years in the convent, she wrote *Life in a Jewish Family*. It did nothing to help the Jews, however, because she died before it could be published.

## The Science of the Cross

After Crystal Night, on November 9, 1938, the evening when the Nazis wreaked havoc and smashed windows in Jewish homes, Edith realized that she was no longer safe in Germany. Her presence in the convent was bringing danger to her Catholic sis-

*To Jews it seems that Christians have "stolen" Edith. After all, she died because she was a Jew, and yet she is claimed as a Christian martyr. But anyone who has read her story knows that, because she was a Christian, Edith turned down chances to leave Germany, convinced that she must embrace the cross of German hatred for the sake of her people, the Jews.*

ters. So, on December 31, 1938, she transferred to Echt in the Netherlands. Soon her sister, Rose, who had also become a Christian, joined her. In Echt, Edith wrote a study of St. John of the Cross called *The Science of the Cross* and taught Jewish Catholic children.

In 1942 the Nazis began deporting Jews from the Netherlands to concentration camps. Edith and Rose applied for Swiss visas. Edith's arrangements were quickly made, but no place could be found for Rose, who was not a nun. Edith could have fled ahead to safety, but loyalty would not allow her to leave her sister.

On July 1, 1942, the Nazis prohibited the education of Jewish Catholic children in the Netherlands. The bishops protested, and in retaliation the Nazis arrested all of the Jewish Catholics. At 5:00 p.m. on Sunday, August 2, while Edith was working on *The Science of the Cross*, two SS officers knocked on the convent door. The sister in charge thought they had come about the visas and sent Edith downstairs to them. Edith was ordered to pack and be ready to leave in five minutes. She was momentarily so dazed that the other nuns had to help her pack. The prioress tried to negotiate with the SS, but without success.

Out in the street a crowd of angry people gathered, calling the act an outrage. Rose grew disoriented. Edith touched her hand and said, "Come, Rosa, we're going for our people."

They were driven at top speed to police headquarters and by midnight were taken to the camp at Amersfoort. All of the captured Jews were driven toward their sleeping quarters amid blows from fists and clubs. Many mothers were in such despair that they could not tend to their own children. Edith at once took care of the little ones, washing and feeding them.

The next night the Steins were taken with 1,200 other Jews to Westerbork. There they were made to walk from table to table filling out meaningless forms as a means of torment. A guard in the Dutch camps said, "[Edith] was in the hell of Westerbork only a few days, walking among the prisoners and talking and praying like a saint . . . a talk with her was like a visit to another world." Again Edith took charge of the children and also did what she could to clean the living quarters. How was she able to do it? She said, "One can only learn the 'Science of the Cross' if one feels the cross in one's own person."

On August 9, 1942, Edith and Rose arrived in Auschwitz. The stench aboard the transport vehicle was awful. Packed into cars like cattle with nowhere to relieve themselves, no food and no water, several prisoners died in transit. Others lost their reason. Edith did not. She was still dressed in her religious habit and easily recognizable. One of the guards remarked, "That one is sane, anyway." The peace that Edith had been so impressed to see in Anna Reinach was now shining through Edith.

The prisoners were ordered to form lines. An SS doctor chose 295 whom he considered fit for work. The rest—Edith, Rose and 262 others—were loaded into trucks and driven to two cottages where they were told to undress so they could shower and be deloused.

Edith entered one of the cottages. It had no windows. Some of the Jews panicked, perhaps guessing what lay in store. They were shoved inside. The few who balked were shot on the spot. Air-tight doors were bolted shut, and Zyklon-B poison was discharged into the room through vents in the ceiling. Within twenty minutes Edith and the rest were dead.

Edith's life and writings, so centered on the cross, have been a deep inspiration to Christians both inside and outside the Catholic Church. In October of 1998, Pope John Paul II canonized her as a saint.

*Recommended reading: Freda Mary Oben,* Edith Stein: Scholar, Feminist, Saint *(New York: Alba House, 1988).*

# TOO LATE WARNING

*I*rene Ferrel was the third child of her parents. It was a
snowy night when she was born in 1921, and, unable to
summon a doctor in time, her anxious father delivered her in
obedience to instructions from his self-possessed wife.

Despite firm discipline from her parents, Irene grew up to be impulsive and fun-loving.
She was an excellent shot with a gun and often brought home game for her family to eat. Her
mother, who had led Irene to Christ, died in 1934, when Irene was only thirteen. The faith
that was planted in Irene as a child was what led her to the Congo and into a night of desperate danger on January 25, 1964.

## Irene Ferrel

**Born:** *December 18, 1921,
in Eagle Butte, SD*
**Education:** *Attended Biola
University*
**Married:** *Did not marry*
**Children:** *None*
**Died:** *January 25, 1964,
in the Congo*
**Quote:** *"May we walk
pleasing unto the Lord
. . . fruitful in every good
word and work."*

## A White Bandage from the Sky

"We fear the beating of the drum for classes is
inciting the *Jeunesse*." Nkedi, the Congolese director of the Baptist Mid-Mission primary school in
Mangungu, spoke with concern. The *Jeunesse*
("youth") were rebels who were notorious for
massacres and torture. They had forced all the village schools to close. Beating a drum (the Congo
school bell) was a daily reminder to the terrorists
that the mission school was still in operation. This
spelled danger for anyone who was associated
with the school, for the Marxist guerrillas considered Christianity to be their most formidable
competitor.

Standing in the shade in front of their house,
missionaries Irene Ferrel and Ruth Hege listened
with sympathy as the African teachers agreed with

*Irene Ferrel was a rather ordinary girl who was raised in an ordinary prairie family at the turn of the century. She was the "ornery" child of the family who got most of the whippings. But, when she gave her heart to Christ, it was for keeps. As a missionary in the Congo, she gave her life too, on one terror-filled night.*

Nkedi that the school should be closed for a few weeks until the threat had passed. As they talked, the whir of an airplane was heard overhead.

*"Avion! Avion! Avion!"* shouted the Africans in the village. Excitement was high because airplanes were the lifeline of the remote mission stations. Everyone ran together as the pilot flung out a packet that trailed a white bandage. The packet fell into some bushes behind the house. Attached was a note.

Opening the letter with trembling fingers, Irene read, "Are you in trouble? All missionaries have been evacuated from Mukedi. Kandala Station burned and missionaries evacuated." The note asked them to signal their intentions. "If you want to be evacuated, sit on the ground. We will send a helicopter for you." The red-and-white Missionary Aviation Fellowship plane circled back to get their response. There was no time for the missionaries to weigh their options. "Lord, lead us," they gasped. They did not want to abandon the African Christians, and yet, as the only two white women in the region, they stuck out as obvious targets, inviting attack. Hand in hand, Irene and Ruth walked to the clearing and sat. The Cessna dipped a wing to show that their reply was understood and zipped away. It was 3:00 p.m. on January 24, 1964, in the Congo (currently known as the Democratic Republic of Congo).

## No Time to Lose

There was no time to lose. No doubt the helicopter would be winging toward them within the hour. "We will be back," the women promised their loyal Congolese friends. Then they hurried to wrap up final details—packing, paying workmen and hiding the car.

The evening brought no helicopter. Christians gathered at the mission station for a farewell service. When the meeting broke up at midnight, Pastor Luka said, "We will be right here. We are not going to our houses to sleep tonight. . . . We want to be here to see the *avion* come down." The women gratefully read between the lines: He and the others were offering to guard them as best they could from the *Jeunesse* that night.

Despite the insurrection that was tearing at the guts of the Congo, the mission station had been so peaceful that even then Irene and Ruth found it hard to believe that they were really in danger. Ruth went to bed, but before she could doze off, the night air carried the urgent cries of Pastor Luka and the others shouting a warning. There was the sound of many running feet.

Shrieks and the crash of broken glass plainly told the women that the *Jeunesse* had come. Ruth leaped up and jerked on her clothes, grabbing her shoes. She rushed to Irene's room. What were they to do?

The *Jeunesse* poured into the house, looting everything, even snatching Ruth's shoes from her hand. Shoving, pulling and shouting, the drug-crazed bandits dragged the two women fifty feet across the lawn. Ruth's skirt was ripped from her with such violence she was almost flung to the ground. She thanked God that she and Irene were still together.

> *You will never know what an influence you have had upon our lives. As I speak and give my testimony of my life, the one thing I like to bring home to people is the fact of a family altar as we had it. I am sure this was the greatest asset in many respects to keep us together as a family in the Lord and us children from going into the world.*
> *—Irene Ferrel*
> *to her father*

An arrow hurtled toward them, plunging into Irene's throat. "I am finished," gasped Irene. She took one step and fell. She was Baptist Mid-Mission's only martyr of the twentieth century.

Crying Irene's name, Ruth collapsed, wounded, beside her and passed out in her blood. When Ruth awoke, the *Jeunesse* were still on the grounds. It was cold and she shivered violently. The *Jeunesse* approached. Seeing Ruth bloody, they thought her dead. A man reached down to feel her. By God's grace, she was able to stop her shuddering. "Dead," said the rebel. Two others repeated the experiment. Finally, they left. Ruth was relieved; a few days before, the *Jeunesse* had hacked up the dead bodies of three priests whom they had killed.

When the *Jeunesse* left, Ruth crawled to a hiding place. The next day, with the help of African Christians, she buried Irene's body without even the charity of a coffin.

The terrorists returned again the next morning and found and captured Ruth. She survived three more days of terror before she was rescued by a United Nations helicopter. (There has never been a good explanation given as to why the rescue did not come

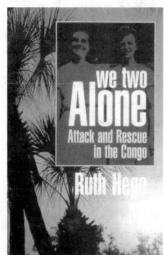

Used by permission of Baptist Mid-Mission

*The book that Ruth Hege wrote about her experience in the Congo*

as soon as promised.) Over the course of those three days, Ruth managed to tell the *Jeunesse* of Christ's love, and the men softened, sparing her life. They promised, however, to destroy the helicopter if it came. Fortunately, the *Jeunesse* left the compound to search the forest for an enemy and were gone when Ruth's rescuers arrived. Pastors Luka and Zechariah, who shielded her, were later tortured, but they escaped and hid in the forest.

## A Kernel of Wheat

After Irene's death, people from around the world asked Ruth whether such a sacrifice was worth any possible rewards. By then, Ruth was able to point to Christians who had determined to follow Christ more closely, men and women who were spurred to go to the mission field, a young man who gave his life to Christ in a prison cell—all because of Irene's story. Was it worth it? Ruth quoted Christ's words: "Unless a kernel of wheat falls to the ground and dies, it remains only a single seed. But if it dies, it produces many seeds" [John 12:24, NIV].

*Recommended reading: Ruth Hege,* We Two Alone: Attack and Rescue in the Congo *(Greenville, SC: Emerald House, 1997).*

# Part 4
## First-Rate Minds

*Their wits*
*left a*
*lasting mark.*

# SYBIL
## *of the*
# RHINE

*H*ow can a middle-aged woman who lives under many restrictions influence her world? For Hildegard, that was an important question. In 1140 the German nun was forty-two and had little education. She was just one unimportant abbess among hundreds who lived in a world run by men. Indeed, it took an extraordinary event—a vision—to force Hildegard onto the public stage:

## Hildegard of Bingen

**Born:** Around 1098 in Bemersheim, Germany
**Education:** Took classes in German convents
**Married:** Did not marry
**Children:** None
**Died:** September 17, 1179, in Rupertsburg, Germany
**Quote:** "Whoever . . . has good qualities, but ascribes them to himself alone . . . is like an infidel."

[H]eaven was opened and a fiery light of exceeding brilliance came and permeated my whole brain, and inflamed my whole heart and my whole breast, not like a burning but a warming flame, as the sun warms anything its rays touch.

Along with the vision, she received a command: "O fragile one, ash of ash and corruption of corruption, say and write what you see and hear." But, although Hildegard continued to receive visions, she did not act. As she explained,

But although I heard and saw these things, because of doubt and a low opinion of myself and because of diverse sayings of men, I refused for a long time a call to write, not out of stubbornness but out of humility, until, weighed down by a scourge of God, I fell onto a bed of sickness.

*On humility: Thus beware lest you attribute to yourself alone those good qualities which are yours in both your spirit and your works. Rather, attribute them to God, from whom all virtues proceed like sparks from a fire. . . . For whoever is aware that he has good qualities, but ascribes them to himself alone, that person is like an infidel who worships only the works of his own hands.*

—*Hildegard's letters*

*When Hildegard recovered from her sickness, she rose up, determined to obey the command that she had neglected. Her first move was to tell her spiritual advisor, the monk Volmar, of the command she had heard and to share some of her visions with him. This was prudent. By getting Volmar's permission to speak, she would avoid bringing the anger of the Church down upon her. She did not want anyone to say out of jealousy that her teachings were demonic or heretical.*

*Volmar was impressed and brought Hildegard's visions to the attention of Church authorities. Abbot Kuno of Disibodenberg gave his permission for her to keep records of her visions. Pope Eugenius, attending a synod held at Trier, read her records and approved them as well. He commanded the nun to write down any further visions that she received from the Holy Spirit and send them to him. Bernard of Clairvaux, the best-known churchman of that day, also praised Hildegard's visions.*

*It is little wonder, in light of these endorsements, that the Church looked to Hildegard as to a prophetess. Her words of counsel in the following years seemed so wise to contemporaries that they nicknamed her the "Sybil of the Rhine."*

## Letters to Medieval Churches

Hildegard's wisdom was sought by many. Archbishop Philip of Cologne was only repeating what most Christians thought when he said that it was common knowledge that Hildegard was "infused with the divine gift of charisma." Adam of Ebra declared that the gift of the Holy Spirit "works many marvels in you [Hildegard] by the spirit of prophecy."

Hildegard was convinced that her wisdom came directly from God. She even wrote letters as if speaking for Him: "Hear therefore the reply not of man, but of Him who lives . . ." or "The Serene Light says . . ."

Letters became Hildegard's principle means of influencing the Church of her day. She was asked for her advice on many matters, and because she understood the people of her day, she answered them sensibly. Hundreds of letters went out to people both high and low: to Emperor Frederick Barbarossa, King Henry II of England, archbishops, bishops, priests, monks and abbesses. Sometimes the letters contained advice, sometimes prophecies, sometimes warnings. "In the solitary life which you seem to be considering you will have no peace because of the instability of your ways, and then your end will be much worse than your beginning," she wrote to a restless abbess. When the city of Mainz tolerated Cathar heretics, she responded with a warning: "The church mourns and wails over their wickedness while her sons are polluted by their iniquity. Therefore cast them from yourselves, lest your community and city perish."

At times Hildegard's pen could be quite sharp. To Abbot Kuno, Hildegard wrote,

> O how foolish is the man who does not amend his own life, and yet
> delves into other people's private affairs and, with a torrent of words
> like rushing waters, noises abroad all the vices he finds hidden there....
> Why do you not examine your own heart and reject your unabashed
> lasciviousness?

For Odo of Soissons she had this to say: "O man, you are like a cloud that shifts back and forth, and no matter where it is, has very little light. And indeed it frequently blocks out the sun, so that its light is cut off for a long time."

The bishop of Prague must have winced at what Hildegard wrote to him:

> Now, O man, you who are wavering and unstable in your character,
> and do not aggressively seek a remedy for yourself and others, rise up
> and look at the sun with due moderation. And do not flee from the light
> or shun it because of the severity of your sins, lest you be ashamed when
> the mighty King examines your works. Then you will live forever.

## Behind Every Great Woman Stands a Woman

It may have taken Hildegard a long time to discover her role in the Church, but she had actually been an unusual person from the very start. Born around 1098, she was the daughter of the nobleman Hildebert of Gut Bermesheim and his wife Mechthilde. As a child, Hildegard was frail of health and had a mystical disposition. After she had become famous, she wrote that she had seen her first vision before she was even five years old.

Perhaps it was Hildegard's ability to see visions that led her parents to "tithe" her to God. At any rate, when she was just eight years old, they walled her up in a cell with her Aunt Jutta of Spanheim, who was a recluse (that is, one who led a solitary life for religious purposes).

Hildegard's isolation was expected to last for life. However, Jutta must have had exceptional qualities herself, because she attracted many other women to join her. The cell be-

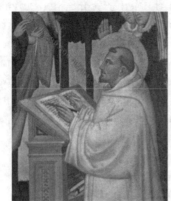

Courtesy Tony Lane

*Bernard of Clairvaux, one of the many prominent individuals who endorsed Hildegard's visions*

came too small to hold them all, and the Benedictine Convent at Disibodenberg (near Mainz, Germany) was built. At age fourteen Hildegard became one of its nuns.

We know little of Hildegard's following years except that she was an assistant to Jutta, who trained her. Jutta must have trained Hildegard well, for when her aunt died in 1136, Hildegard was chosen to be abbess in Jutta's place. Hildegard was thirty-eight years old.

## Making Big Opportunities Bigger

All of Hildegard's memorable contributions came after she assumed the leadership of the convent. This is not surprising. While she had been under Jutta's hand, Hildegard had to follow her aunt's direction and guidance. However, once she herself was the superior at the convent, she could make decisions on her own, as well as find expression for her talents in many new spheres, and she seized the opportunity. She was able to act boldly on the ideas that came to her, although she still had to get approval from the men who supervised the nuns.

She began by recruiting new nuns. Their numbers grew too large for the old convent, so she set out to build a bigger facility in a different location. This plan met with murmurs from some of her nuns, who liked their comforts and did not want to leave them. Hildegard, however, had a deeper motivation: She wanted to reduce male supervision over her convent and gain more freedom of action. The place she picked for the new convent was not as easy for the monks to supervise. She personally oversaw construction at Rupertsberg, near Bingen, Germany. After she moved to the new convent in 1150, she became known as Hildegard of Bingen.

## Know the Way

Around 1141, Hildegard began to write her book *Scivias* (or *Sciens Vias*, "Know the Way"), which took her ten years to complete. The book included twenty-six drawings of things she saw in her wide-awake visions. Modern medicine suggests that these shimmering lines of light were actually the auras associated with migraines. Hilde- gard's own account suggests more, however. She claimed, "Suddenly I understood the meaning of the expositions of the . . . Old and New Testaments." She probably would not have been fooled by migraines because she was well aware of their effects and wrote, "When headache and migraine and vertigo attack a patient simultaneously, they render a man foolish and upset his reason."

The men and women of her day were persuaded that Hildegard understood past, present and future. The man who wrote her life story said that even as an infant she had astonished others with her confusing utterances of things that later came true.

*The story of Hildegard's life, once known only to scholars, has undergone a revival of interest in recent years. Her music has been recorded, her letters translated, her visions examined medically and her biography written. By all accounts she was one of the most extraordinary women of her era.*

After *Scivias*, Hildegard wrote other books of visions, the *Book of Life's Merits* and the *Book of the Divine Works*. She challenged the male world by writing in Latin, the language of educated men, although she had never been formally trained in it.

## Medicine and Mental Illness

In medieval Europe, monasteries and convents were the closest equivalent to hospitals, and when medical responsibilities settled upon Hildegard, her active mind directed her to ferret out medical lore. She compiled *Causae et Curae*, a book rich with prescriptions to guide treatment of the sick. She identified and described mental illnesses such as despair, dread, frenzy, insanity and obsession. Symptoms that she used for medical diagnoses included redness or paleness of the face, the brightness of blood, the smell of a person's breath, coughs, degrees of fever, changes in the pulse and changes in urine and feces. Her medicine included exorcisms, herbal lore and much medieval nonsense, such as the belief that gems could cure sickness.

Hildegard was also interested in physical phenomena, and she gathered many details about nature into an encyclopedic work titled *Physica* ("Natural History"). According to historians of the sciences, her work included original observations and put her on par with the top naturalists of her day.

## Stretching the Bounds of Literature

Courtesy Charles Singer, *From Magic to Science* (London: Ernest Benn, 1928)

*"The New Heavens and the New Earth and the New Ordering of the Elements" from* Scivias

Books were rare in those days, and Bibles were almost nonexistent. If the majority of laypeople were to be taught about the Christian life, it had to be through verbal instruction. Like every good teacher, Hildegard knew that oral instruction was made more memorable if it was presented in imaginative and interesting forms. The Church had long used visual and musical aids in worship, and the Catholic Mass included both. As a leader of religious services, Hildegard developed her own aids. She prepared hymns and singing responses to be included in the services. She wrote the first morality play (a play in which people, given the names of virtues, contend with the devil) known to have been set to music (it was probably written around 1150 for the dedication of the new abbey). In *Play of the Virtues*, Hildegard reversed the usual order of things by giving women the parts of the virtues and making a man play the devil's role.

Over the course of her lifetime, Hildegard composed seventy vocal works. The worth of those works was rediscovered only in the 1980s, and some have now been recorded. Hildegard not only composed the music for those works but also wrote their lyrics. One song cycle she composed reveals her hunger for Christ: "It is very hard to resist what tastes of the apple. Set us upright Savior, Christ. . . . O most beautiful form! O most sweet savor of desirable delight! We ever sigh after you in fearful exile, when will we see you and dwell with you?"

## Not a Retiring Person

Around 1158, at the age of sixty, when most people would contemplate retirement, Hildegard undertook the first of several preaching tours. Women seldom were allowed to teach the opposite sex, but Hildegard was allowed to preach to men. This shows just how much respect she had gained.

She taught in her sermons that the Church was corrupt and needed cleansing. She raked easy-going, fat clergymen over the coals with her tongue and chewed out those who were "lukewarm and sluggish" in serving God's justice or negligent in expounding the depths of Scripture.

Hildegard died at age eighty-two on September 17, 1179. By force of character, she had overcome the limitations that restricted women during the Middle Ages. She seized her opportunities, stretched her limits and became one of the most influential women of the medieval era.

*Recommended reading: Sabina Flanagan,* Hildegard of Bingen, 1098-1179: A Visionary Life *(London: Routledge, 1989).*

# APOSTLE
## *to the*
# POOR

*W*hen Hannah More was an old woman, dishonest servants took advantage of her frailty and robbed her. Her friends feared for her safety and came to get her. As she came downstairs to meet them, she proved that she had not lost her wit: "I am driven like Eve out of Paradise," she said, "but not like Eve by angels."

## Hannah More

**Born:** *February 2, 1745, in Stapleton, Gloucestershire*

**Education:** *Taught at home and attended language schools*

**Married:** *Did not marry*

**Children:** *None*

**Died:** *September 7, 1833, in Clifton, England*

**Quote:** *"I have been a great sinner, but He [Christ] has told me tho my sins are as scarlet they are become as wool."*

## Forgotten Flower

Though probably the most well-known and influential woman in England during her day and the friend of scholar Samuel Johnson, actor David Garrick and abolitionist William Wilberforce, Hannah More is almost forgotten today. Who was this now-obscure woman who counted so many leaders and prominent persons among her friends?

Born in Stapleton (near Bristol, England) in 1745, Hannah was the fourth in a family of five girls. Her father, Jacob More, was a schoolmaster who saw to it that his daughters were well-educated. While still in their teens, the three oldest More daughters established a girls' boarding school in Bristol that soon became famous. Hannah completed her education there, and before she was eighteen she wrote *A Search for Happiness*, a play that was later published and widely read.

In 1772 Hannah took her first of many trips to London, where she became a figure of social and

*An admirer named Edward Turner courted Hannah for six years and proposed to her. She accepted his offer, but twice he got cold feet and called off the ceremony. After he reneged a third time, Hannah ended the engagement. Turner then insisted on making material provision for her. Hannah rejected the offered money, but behind her back her sisters accepted the payment. Consequently, Hannah had the comfortable income of £200 in her later years; she eventually agreed to use it.*

literary importance, enjoying the company and friendship of artist Sir Joshua Reynolds and statesman Edmund Burke. The famous actor David Garrick himself directed her successful play *Percy*, and John Wesley wrote to Hannah to encourage her in her literary pursuits, saying that her Christian example could greatly influence the London artistic and literary set. However, when Garrick and Doctor Samuel Johnson (the author for whom that literary period, the Age of Johnson, was named) died, London society lost its glamour and interest for Hannah. She felt guilty for having written plays, unsure that acting was an activity that a Christian should endorse, no matter how moral the play's contents.

In her early years, Hannah had not been adverse to the high life. She kept up a lively correspondence with others and was part of every festivity. And, to the end of her days she was on easy terms with "infidels" such as Horace Walpole. After 1785, however, she increasingly turned toward more distinctly Christian work. Pastor John Newton, author of "Amazing Grace," became her spiritual advisor, and young William Wilberforce, leader in the abolition movement, became her close friend. Members of the Clapham Sect, a group of well-to-do Anglican evangelicals, also became Hannah's friends and supporters.

## Writing with a Moral Purpose

All of Hannah's writings were permeated with a strong moral purpose. She wrote a series of popular essays on the importance of Christianity in establishing moral laws, as well as a series of popular tracts to counter the rationalism of the French Revolution. The most famous of her works, *The Shepherd of Salisbury Plain*, written around 1795, went through many editions and was translated into several languages. Like many of her tracts, it called commoners to be content with their lot.

In 1809 Hannah published a widely read novel titled *Coelebs in Search of a Wife*, which was really an essay on how to choose a good wife. It went through thirty editions in the

United States within ten years. Her *Strictures on the Modern System of Female Education* encouraged education for women based on a foundation of Christian teaching and morals.

## Sunday Schools for Miners

Hannah lived during the heyday of the Sunday school system. Appalled at the poverty and immorality in mining towns, in 1789 she and her sisters began to establish Sunday schools in the brutal coal district of Mendip Hills, where atrocities had turned humans almost into animals. Within ten years the Mores were supporting and administering over sixteen schools, helping the poor children to read the Scriptures, learn Christian morals and acquire skills that would help them through life. Firmly believing that Christian teaching should be the basis of all education, Hannah wrote many of the books that were used in the Sunday schools.

The miners desperately needed knowledge in order to improve their lives; they did not even know how to use the little money they had. Most did not know how to grow vegetables to supplement their tables or how to cook them when they had them. Hannah's homemaking classes addressed such practicalities.

There was, however, terrific opposition to Hannah's schools from the clergy and mine owners in the town. The gentry feared that men who could read the Bible could also read propaganda. They were right—and wrong. The good done by exposing the masses to the Scriptures was immense. Many of them developed Christ-centered lives as a result.

## Useful Even in Death

Toward the end of her life, Hannah, whose days had been a whirlwind of activity, became weak and had to limit her visits with others to two days a week. But her vivacity, wit and charity evoked love from the rising generation. She died peacefully on September 7, 1833, at the age of eighty-eight. She had spent much of her life improving the con-

> *The shepherd and his wife sat down with great seeming cheerfulness, but the children stood; and while mother was helping them, little fresh-colored Molly . . . cried out, "Father, I wish I was big enough to say grace, I am sure I would say it very heartily today, for I was thinking what must poor people do who have no salt for their potatoes; and do but look, our dish is quite full.*
> —from The Shepherd of Salisbury Plain

dition of many other people's lives. Even in death, she made herself useful. Most of the £30,000 she left behind was bequeathed to churches and charities.

*Recommended reading: Mary Alden Hopkins,* Hannah More and Her Circle *(New York: Longman, Green, 1947).*

# LITTLE LADY, BIG WAR

*I*n Harriet's pocket was $100 and a plea from Gamaliel Bailey, asking her to write an antislavery story for his magazine, National Era. *Bailey had printed several of Harriet's antislavery articles already. In an 1850 article titled "The Freeman's Dream," she had written of a farmer who was judged by Christ for refusing to give bread to a runaway slave because of the Fugitive Slave Act. In the story, Jesus says to the man, "Depart from me, ye accursed, for I was an hungered and ye gave me no meat."*

*The Fugitive Slave Act made Harriet's blood boil. It ordered citizens to aid in arresting and returning runaway slaves to the South. Anyone who gave food or shelter to an escaping slave was subject to a $1,000 fine. Under this act, fear reigned in white and black people alike, and terrible outrages were perpetrated. A black waiter named Henry Long had been violently seized at the Pacific Hotel in New York because he had been "claimed" by John T. Smith of Richmond, Virginia. Despite the fact that Henry had worked at the hotel long before the alleged date of his escape, he was sent South. "Is it possible that . . . in all this nation of freemen there is not one deliverer brave enough and strong enough to rescue him?" raged Harriet.*

*Harriet's sister Isabella wrote her a letter from Boston describing several outrages that were perpetrated under the act. "Now, Hattie, if I could use my pen as you can," Isabella wrote, "I would write something that would make this whole nation feel what an accursed thing slavery is." Harriet read the letter and rose from her chair. "I will write something," she said. "I will if I live."*

## Harriet Beecher Stowe

**Born:** June 14, 1811, in Litchfield, CT

**Education:** Attended Litchfield Academy and her sister's school in Hartford, CT

**Married:** Calvin Stowe in January 1836

**Children:** Seven

**Died:** July 1, 1896

**Quote:** "Are we ready to take the exceeding and eternal weight of glory?"

*When one of Harriet's children died, her critics said that God had taken the baby to keep Harriet from growing vain over her success with Uncle Tom's Cabin. Stung, she replied, "I wrote what I did because as a woman, as a mother, I was oppressed and broken-hearted, with the sorrows and injustice I saw, because as a Christian I felt the dishonor to Christianity—because as a lover of my country I trembled at the coming day of wrath."*

## Uncle Tom's Cabin

"I will write," Harriet had promised. But the autumn of 1850 gave way to winter, and still she had made no start on the story. Her mind was blank. Night after night she sat in front of her fire thinking, but no idea came to her.

Then February rolled around, and one cold Sunday morning as Harriet attended a communion service, a vision formed in her mind. She saw an old slave undergoing a brutal beating and forgiving his tormentors as he prayed for them. Harriet accepted it as a vision directly from the Lord. It was a miracle! She hurried home from church and wrote down the scenes as she had seen them. As soon as she was done, she summoned her hungry children—dinner had been suspended while she wrote—and read aloud what she had written. "Oh, Mama," sobbed one. "Slavery is the most cruel thing in the world!"

Ideas fell into Harriet's mind like snowflakes in a blizzard. She saw that she would need to write a full novel to tell the story. She suggested that Bailey publish the story in installments, and he agreed. And so *Uncle Tom's Cabin* was written and printed in parts between the years 1851 and 1852.

## About the Author

Harriet was born in Litchfield, Connecticut, on June 14, 1811, the seventh child of Lyman Beecher. "Wisht it had been a boy," the Calvinist preacher had remarked. Although he doted on his daughters, he would have preferred for Harriet to be a son who could follow him into the pulpit.

Harriet was just four when her shy, blushing mother died. Devastated, Lyman described himself as like a child shut out in the dark, and Harriet never forgot those words. The responsibilities of the household fell upon fifteen-year-old Catherine, the oldest of the Beecher daughters. From then on, Harriet turned to Catherine as to a mother in times of trouble, and the two exchanged letters all of their lives.

By age six Harriet was reading adult books, but she hated writing. That soon changed, however. One of the greatest triumphs of her life came when she was twelve and she saw her father's face brighten when an essay on immortality was read anonymously. How Lyman beamed when the essay won first prize and he learned that it was his daughter's. She treasured that moment of approval more than the success of any of her later stories.

In spite of her aptitude for reading, Harriet found it hard to understand her father's sermons. They might as well have been written in Choctaw (a Native American language) for all the good she got from them, she said. And his Calvinist God seemed unfair to her. But one day when she was fourteen, "a certain pathetic earnestness in his voice" caused her to listen to the sermon more closely than usual. She began to cry. When they came home from church, she told her father that she had given herself wholeheartedly to Christ.

Courtesy Charles Edward Stowe and Lyman Beecher Stowe, *Harriet Beecher Stowe* (Boston: Houghton Mifflin, 1911)

### Calvin Stowe

In 1836 Harriet married the Bible scholar Calvin Stowe, who proved to be an indecisive man, constantly changing his mind as to where he wanted to live or teach. Harriet thought he lacked Christian fervor and wrote to him, "If you had studied Christ with half the energy that you have studied Luther . . . then would He be formed in you." After one of their children died, Harriet and Calvin turned to spiritualism, attending séances at which psychics claimed to put loved ones in contact with their dead, but Harriet soon saw that it was wrong and reminded her husband that it was an unbiblical practice. Unfortunately, she could not persuade him to give it up.

## Little Lady, Big War

Meanwhile, John P. Jewett of Boston bought the book rights to *Uncle Tom's Cabin* in 1852. A week after Harriet signed the contract, the novel was in stores. Overnight, it became a best-seller. In its first year, 120 editions were printed. Harriet had received $300 for the version that Bailey had printed in his magazine; her first royalty check for the book was for $10,000. No American novel had sold like it—350,000 copies in 12 months. Within two years the book was translated into seventeen languages, including Siamese.

*It [Uncle Tom's Cabin] knew the large felicity of gathering in alike the small and the simple and the big and the wise . . . much less a book than a vision.*

—Henry James

Harriet thought that she had written a conciliatory book. Most of the slave owners in the story were shown as kindly people who were trapped within a system they had not created. Radical abolitionists, willing to use any means to rid the nation of the curse of slavery, were, in her eyes, more detestable than slave owners. Contrary to Harriet's expectations, however, the book heightened the anger of the South, who said that the book was full of lies and that it inflamed the antislavery emotions of the North. Abraham Lincoln believed that it triggered the Civil War. When he met Harriet during the war, he remarked, "So this is the little lady who made this big war!"

Although Harriet wrote many other books and stories, *Uncle Tom's Cabin* was her best. She tried to portray black people as fully human, and more important, as men and women who had been made in the image of Christ.

The book did have its faults. She could at times be patronizing, such as when she wrote, "In order to appreciate the sufferings of the negroes sold south, it must be remembered that all the instinctive affections of that race are particularly strong. Their local attachments are very abiding. They are not naturally daring and enterprising, but home-loving and affectionate." This type of stereotyping has led some African Americans to use "Uncle Tom" as a scornful name for any African American who accepts his conditions as they are.

Another perceived fault with Harriet's writing is that her descriptions, such as that of Augustine St. Clare, were perhaps too long, some running to several pages. Most irritating to a modern reader might be her tendency to stop and talk directly to him or her: "And oh! mother that reads this, has there never been in your house a drawer, or a closet, the opening of which has been to you like the opening again of a little grave? Ah! happy mother that you are, if it has not been so."

Some critics call the book "trash" or "sentimental drivel" because of these obvious faults, but many writers of Harriet's day wrote in the same way. It is likely that the "fault" that certain readers secretly found the most irritating was Harriet's frequent introduction of religion and Scripture onto her pages—words such as, "Depend upon it, God will bring you into judgment for this."

Today *Uncle Tom's Cabin* is acknowledged as an outstanding work of American fiction, perhaps even the nation's greatest book, especially notable for its vivid character portraits. The characters of Uncle Tom, Simon Legree, Eva and Topsy are unforgettable. The image of Eliza crossing the Ohio River by leaping from chunk to chunk of ice is an indelible picture that was based on a true story.

## Clearing Lady Byron's Name

Harriet's strong sense of justice brought her to a decision in 1868 to publish an article in defense of her dead friend Lady Byron, whose motives for leaving her famous poet husband were being impugned. Lady Byron had confided the facts to Harriet when she visited Lady Byron in England in 1856. Harriet's "True Story of Lady Byron's Life" appeared in the *Atlantic Monthly*. In it, she accused Lord Byron of serious misconduct with his half sister, Augusta Leigh. Lord Byron had also renounced Christianity and jeered at his wife's hopes to reform him.

Courtesy Lord Macaulay et al., *The True Story of Lord and Lady Byron* (London: John Camden Hotten, 1869)

### Lady Byron

Harriet's allegations were true, but the press angrily said that she had breached good taste. Individuals corroborated Harriet's facts, but circulation of the *Atlantic Monthly* dropped seriously as a result of the article. Augusta admitted to the incestuous relationship, but Harriet could not win back her public after the incident. The author of *Uncle Tom's Cabin* lost her mind in her old age and lived in a dream world for several years as she drifted toward death.

Whatever critics said, Harriet wielded her pen as an instrument for justice. Her book evokes a powerful emotional response from the reader, something that many authors only wish they could do. *Uncle Tom's Cabin* remains a testimony to the power of a Christian writer who tried to expose evil with honest art.

*Recommended reading: Noel B. Gerson,* Harriet Beecher Stowe: A Biography *(New York: Praeger, 1976).*

# FIRST FEMALE PANDIT

"*Women have no minds. They are lower than pigs.*" This was the belief of many of the men in nineteenth-century India. However, one man who did not subscribe to this belief was Ananta Shatri Dongree, a wealthy Hindu guru. He believed that women were intelligent and valuable.

What made Ananta different? One day while he was tutoring in a palace, he heard an Indian princess reciting Sanskrit verses, and he was astonished. Women weren't supposed to be able to learn! Upon realizing that women could learn just as well as men, he made up his mind that when he married, he would teach his wife to read the ancient Hindu scriptures.

Like most Hindu men, Ananta married a little girl. He took his child-wife home to his mother. He began to teach his wife, but his mother refused to allow it. (Under Hindu custom, the older woman was the absolute boss of the younger.) Ananta fled with his wife, Laxmibai, into the Gungamul forest of southern India, where he built a house and taught his wife Sanskrit without interference.

It was there in a crude house in the forest that Ramabai was born in 1858. When she was old enough to learn, her mother taught her the Hindu scriptures, and by the time Ramabai was twenty, she could recite from memory 18,000 verses of the Puranas, a Hindu holy book. She learned to speak English as well as many of India's dialects, including Marathi, Bengali, Hindustani and Kanarese.

## Pandita Ramabai

**Born:** April 1858 in southern India

**Education:** Taught at home

**Married:** Babu Bipen Beharidas Medhavi in October 1880

**Children:** One daughter

**Died:** April 5, 1922

**Quote:** "This faithful text [1 Thessalonians 5:24] has been written with the life-blood of Christ on my heart."

पंडिता रमाबाई
(1858-1920)

अनन्त शास्त्री की सबसे छोटी पुत्री पंडिता रमाबाई एक समाज सुधारक, महिला उद्धार की समर्थक और शिक्षा के क्षेत्र में एक अग्रणी महिला थी। मात्र 23 वर्ष की आयु में नितान्त एकाकी रह जाने वाली रमाबाई ने एक संस्कृत विदुषी के रूप में अत्यधिक ख्याति अर्जित की।

कलकत्ता विश्वविद्यालय के संस्कृत विद्वानों ने उनकी योग्यता से अत्यधिक प्रभावित होकर उन्हें "सरस्वती" और "पंडिता" की उपाधियों से विभूषित किया। जलसे

Courtesy Christian History Institute Archives

*Sanskrit*

*God was preparing Ramabai for a great work. At the very least, she had already proven that a woman's mind is not inferior to a man's.*

## No Common Sense

Ananta was regarded as wise and holy, and even in the forest students flocked to him. Yet he lived without peace. In 1858, the year of Ramabai's birth, he set out on a pilgrimage with his family to seek the happiness that had so far eluded him. About the pilgrimage Ramabai wrote:

> [W]e had no common sense and foolishly spent all the money we had in hand in giving alms . . . to please the gods, who we thought, would send a shower of gold mohurs upon us and make us rich and happy. We went to several sacred places and temples, to worship different gods and to bathe in sacred rivers and tanks to free ourselves from sin and curse, which brought poverty on us. We prostrated ourselves before the stone and metal images of the gods, and prayed before them day and night; the burden of our prayer being that the gods would be pleased to give us wealth, learning and renown. . . . But nothing came of all this futile effort to please the gods—the stone images remained as hard as ever, and never answered our prayers.

When Ananta's money ran out, the priests, who had been welcoming and friendly before, coldly turned Ananta and his family away with empty bellies. Ananta and his family could not beg without breaking caste and bringing disgrace on their name, so they went for days without food.

Ananta decided to drown himself, an acceptable practice in Hinduism. He gathered his wife and children and bade them farewell. Ramabai remembered the event with pain:

> Though his blind eyes could see me no longer, he held me tightly in his arms, and stroking my head and cheeks, told me, in a few words broken by emotion, to remember how he loved me, how he had taught me to do right, and never to depart from the way of righteousness. His last loving command to me was to lead an honorable life if I lived at all, and to serve God all my life. He did not know the only true God, but served the—to him—unknown God with all his heart and strength; and he was desirous

that his children should serve Him to the last. "Remember, my child," he said, "you are my youngest and most beloved child. I have given you into the hand of our God; you are His, and to Him alone you must belong, and serve Him all your life."

Ananta starved to death before he could drown himself, and he was soon followed by Ramabai's mother and a sister. Ramabai and her brother wandered for 4,000 miles more, hoping to find favor with the gods. Instead they suffered cold, hunger and thirst. They tested the promises of their faith and found them to be unreliable. Finally, they gave up their search for salvation and settled in Calcutta in 1878.

*For the sake of aiding India's widows, Ramabai became a scholar, poet, teacher, farmer, translator, architect, revivalist, author, linguist and manager. Not only was she honored with the title "Pandita," she was also called "Sarasvati" after the goddess of eloquence.*

## The First Woman Pandit

Ramabai's immense knowledge impressed the local Hindu scholars, and they called her "Pandita," which means "learned." She was the first woman ever awarded this title. When they asked her to lecture to their wives on the duties of high-caste Hindu women and she studied the Hindu scriptures—which had formerly been denied to her—in preparation, Ramabai found that the books disagreed on everything "except that women are worse than demons." She could not believe this, because her father had taught her otherwise.

It was in Calcutta that Ramabai first heard about Christ. She discovered that salvation is a free gift from God, not something earned by pilgrimages or greasing the palms of priests. At first she thought that Christians had to live like Europeans. She did not want to eat European foods or wear their clothes, so she joined a cult that fused Christian and Hindu ideas. She escaped from this group only after a Baptist missionary showed her that the way of Christ allowed her freedom to eat and dress as she pleased.

Meanwhile, Ramabai's brother died in May of 1880. Ramabai had married, but her husband died of cholera. She was left with no one in the world but a baby daughter, whom she named Manoramabai, "Heart's Joy."

## "Hells on Earth"

If women ranked low in India, widows ranked even lower. Some were burned alive on their husbands' funeral pyres. Many who were allowed to live were forced to become slaves,

*Some years ago I was brought to the conviction that mine was only an intellectual belief—a belief in which there was no life. . . . God showed me . . . what a wretched and lost sinner I was; and how necessary it was to obtain salvation in the present, and not in some future time. . . . I prayed earnestly to God to pardon my sins for the sake of Jesus Christ and let me realize that I had really got salvation through Him. I believed God's promise and took Him at His word; and when I had done this, my burden rolled away, and I realized that I was forgiven and freed from the power of sin.*

*—Ramabai*

and others were sent to temples to become prostitutes and make money for the priests. Ramabai had seen all of this firsthand. Moving in reform circles as she did, she was spared the worst of this treatment. Nonetheless, she could sympathize with those who were not so fortunate as she. She wrote:

> There are thousands of priests and men learned in sacred lore. . . . They neglect and oppress the widows, and devour widows' houses. . . . They send out hundreds of emissaries to look for young widows, and bring them by hundreds and thousands to the sacred cities to rob them of their money and their virtue . . . and then, after robbing them of their belongings, tempt them to yield to their unholy desires. They shut the young helpless widows into their large [monasteries], sell and hire them out to wicked men so long as they can get money; and when the poor, miserable slaves are no longer pleasing to their cruel masters, they turn them out in the street to beg their livelihood, to suffer the horrible consequences of sin, to carry the burden of shame, and finally to die the death worse than that of a starved street dog! The so-called sacred places—those veritable hells on earth—have become the grave-yards of countless widows and orphans.

Ramabai had already founded an organization to reform the treatment of women in India before her brother died. In 1882 she gave testimony to a reform commission and tried to open a home for widows. Unable to raise funds, she felt that God was nudging her to go to England. Though she had no money, she went in 1883, taking her daughter with her. In Wantage, England, nuns from the Church of England took her in, taught her about Christ and baptized her. Later, Ramabai said that God had led her into a strange land just as He led Abraham into a country he did not know.

Ramabai then traveled to the United States in 1886, where she studied teaching methods and spoke to Christians about India's needs. She published an influential book, *The High Caste Hindu Woman*. Interested Americans formed an organization to support her.

Once back in India in 1889, Ramabai began by opening a school for a few pupils. She promised not to pressure Hindu girls to become Christians. However, she made the Bible available to them. Through reading the Bible and observing Ramabai's godly life, several girls converted to Christianity, and the Hindus complained that Ramabai was betraying her own culture. Eventually Ramabai saw that she could not walk between two different faiths, and she declared that her school would be completely Christian.

## A Refuge Called Mukti

Other projects followed. Many women came to her—girl brides who had been so abused that they were terrified of a touch, older women who snarled like animals from years of cruelty. In 1889, on farm land that had been inherited from her family and land that she bought from a liquor dealer, Ramabai created a refuge called Mukti, which means "salvation." There she taught arts that women could use to support themselves, and she cultivated orchards. In famine, Mukti fed thousands who otherwise would have starved.

Other girl widows, however, refused to come to Mukti. Their minds were filled with dread toward Christians.

> They think that some day after they are well fattened they will be hung
> head downward, and a great fire will be built underneath, and oil will
> be extracted from them to be sold at a fabulously large price for medical
> purposes. Others think that they will be put into mills and their bones
> ground. . . . The minds of the new ones are filled with more dreadful
> ideas than these. They cannot understand that anyone would be kind
> to them without some selfish purpose.

## Holy Burning

Throughout the history of the Church, there have been times when the Holy Spirit moved in God's people and they were awakened to their spiritual conditions. In 1904 this happened in Australia and Wales. Ramabai prayed for the same thing to happen among her own girls. Five hundred and fifty women met daily at Mukti to ask God to come close to them.

Courtesy James S. Dennis, *Christian
Missions and Social Progress* (New
York: Fleming H. Revell, 1909)

*Widows with Ramabai
(in white)*

On June 29, 1905, the Spirit came upon a large
group of girls. Weeping, they confessed their sins.
The next day the Holy Spirit returned with even
greater effect. Girls testified to a holy burning inside
them that was almost unbearable. They counted it a
privilege to spend long hours praying for people they
had never met.

Ramabai so wanted all of India to know the joy
of God's presence that she prayed for 100,000
Christians who could go out and share the gospel
with others. Soon afterward, she was asked to provide food and shelter for 25,000 orphans. She saw
this as the first installment of God's answer and
set herself to the task of training them as children
of the faith.

## Not Lower Than Pigs

Several years before her death in 1922, Ramabai
asked that her name be disassociated from the organizations she led. "Ramabai is dead," she said.
Her work was to be God's alone. Nonetheless, the
work God started by her hands lives on.

Some consider Pandita Ramabai to have been the greatest woman of nineteenth-
century India. Indian philosopher Vishal Mangalwadi summed up her achievements
by calling her India's "Woman of the Millenium." She had come a long way from the
rough forest home her father built before her birth.

*Recommended reading: Helen S. Dyer,* Pandita Ramabai: The
Story of Her Life *(New York: Revell, 1911).*

# Part 5
## She Stooped to Conquer

*They relinquished
fame, prestige and
position for Christ.*

# ELIZABETH
## *of*
# MANY CASTLES

*T*o look at her, you would not have guessed that Elizabeth of Hungary was the daughter of a king and the wife
of a prince. In place of the rich, beautiful dresses of her youth, she
wore the plain gray robe of a Franciscan. Rather than be waited on, she washed lepers with
her own hands. Instead of rich meats and pastries, she ate bread with a little honey or a dry
crust with a small glass of wine. She worked wool like any peasant girl. A Magyar knight who
saw Elizabeth sitting by her little cottage in 1228 exclaimed in astonishment, "Whoever has
seen a king's daughter spinning before?"

## Elizabeth of Hungary

**Born:** *1207 in Bratislavia*

**Education:** *Educated at
Wartburg Castle*

**Married:** *Count Ludwig
IV of Thuringia in 1221*

**Children:** *At least three*

**Died:** *November 17, 1231,
at Marburg, Hesse (in
modern-day Germany)*

**Quote:** *"The world with
all its joys is now dead
to me."*

## Noble Beginnings

Elizabeth von Thuringia was born in 1207 in
the royal castle of Pozsony (Bratislavia, Czecho-
slovakia). Her mother, Gertrude, was a Christian who came from a long line of Christians,
and she imparted her own faith to her daughter.
Elizabeth's father, Andrew II, fought valiantly in
the Crusades, but he was not an exemplary king.
His nobles forced him to sign the Golden Bull in
1222, which was Thuringia's (Hungary) version
of the Magna Carta, limiting the power of the
king and giving more rights to his nobles. Elizabeth's Aunt Hedwig, who founded a convent for
lepers, her Aunt Mechthild, who became abbess
of Kitzingen, and her Uncle Egbert, who was
bishop of Bamberg, all set examples of faith for
their niece.

When she was not yet two, Elizabeth was betrothed to the son of a nobleman who lived in Thuringia, which was then part of the German Empire. At four years of age, Elizabeth was sent to live with her prospective in-laws to be raised according to their customs. Within the thick gray walls of Wartburg Castle, with its parapets, iron gates, watchtowers and drawbridge, Elizabeth grew to womanhood as the playmate of her fiancé and his brother Ludwig IV (Louis IV). No doubt she played more often in the lovely meadows and gardens outside the castle than in the damp cellars below.

When Elizabeth was seven, her mother was murdered in a political assassination. The grieving daughter was old enough to understand that she had a comforter in God, and she knelt in the Wartburg chapel, praying for the souls of the murderers. Shortly after, Elizabeth's fiancé also died.

Her status in Thuringia became unclear, but Ludwig, her fiancé's brother, said that he would like to marry her. Ludwig eased Elizabeth's sorrows, for he was fond of his bride-to-be, and whenever he visited the city, he would bring her some small present, such as a pair of gloves or a new rosary.

## Elizabeth's Dream Day

When Elizabeth was just fourteen years old, her dream day came. In spite of attempts by Ludwig's family to send the beautiful, olive-skinned girl away, declaring her too holy to make a suitable bride for Ludwig, she was married to him as planned in a ceremony held in St. George's Church in Eisenach in 1221. Elizabeth listened well as the bishop read the ceremony and understood that, although she was entering a union with her husband, she could in some sense also experience a mystical union with Christ. In time she would find Christ to be her truest beloved. Meanwhile, she and Ludwig bound themselves to rule justly and to open their home in hospitality to monks and nuns. Ludwig was a young man of noble mind who took as his motto "Piety, Chastity, Justice." Elizabeth adored him.

Elizabeth brought great wealth into the marriage, and by marriage she gained even more. She had the choice of five castles in which to live and was called "Elizabeth of Many Castles." Wealth did not impress her, however. Although she dressed handsomely, she said that she did so only to please her husband so that he might be protected from the temptation to break his wedding vows.

They lived at first on the Danube, and Elizabeth rode across the shattered nation with Ludwig, viewing firsthand the devastation left by the Golden Bull revolt of the Thuringian nobles. When she became pregnant, she moved to Kreutsberg Castle, and it was there in 1222 that her son, Herman, was born. At his birth, Elizabeth took Herman in her arms and walked barefoot to St. Katherine's chapel, where she recited Psalm 127:3: "Children are an

heritage of the LORD: and the fruit of the womb is his
reward." She eventually did the same for two other
children, consecrating them to the Lord.

## Embracing a New Order

Courtesy Christian History Institute archives

*Wartburg Castle, one of*
*Elizabeth's several homes*

St. Francis of Assisi was preaching in Italy in
those days, calling people to repent, cast aside the
chains of wealth and show kindness to the poor
and lepers. Franciscans arrived in Thuringia in
1221, and their message stirred Elizabeth. It corre-
sponded with the goodness she had learned from
her parents. She longed to share her own blessings
with the poor, so, placing herself under the instruction of Brother Rodeger, she opened eastern
Europe's first orphanage and tended to lepers, un-
dertaking their care with her own hands.

This outraged her in-laws. According to one legend, Elizabeth even laid a leper in
her husband's bed. "Come, my son," said her mother-in-law to Ludwig. "You shall see
one of the wonders your Elizabeth works and I cannot prevent." When she flung back
the covers, Ludwig did not see the leper but rather Jesus lying on the bed.

Whether the legend is true or not, Elizabeth's husband did give her funds with which to
establish a leprosarium below Wartburg Castle around 1226 so that weak lepers would not
have to struggle up the castle path, which was so steep that it was called "the knee-smasher."
She poured relief upon all who were in true distress, giving tools with which to work to the
able-bodied and beds to the dying. Ludwig defended Elizabeth's good works against his
family's criticism, saying that such deeds would bring blessing upon the country.

## "Excessive" Generosity

In 1226 severe famine raged in Thuringia, and on its heels came crime and disease.
Ludwig was away, and Elizabeth feared that the people might revolt, for they were so
desperate for food that they had to grind up pine bark as a substitute for flour. When
they crowded against the castle gate, crying for food, she ordered her storehouses to be
emptied for them and ran the ovens day and night, baking bread. With the help of monks
and nuns, she set up soup kitchens across the country. Churches were thrown open to
house the homeless, and she had firewood distributed among the weak. To the fury of her
grasping in-laws, she took all the ready money in the treasury and distributed it among

*A*mong those who told Elizabeth's story in paintings were Fra Angelico, Hans Holbien the Younger, Murillo and Simone Martini. She was written about too. Charles Kingsley, novelist and author of The Water Babies, wrote a poetic drama of Elizabeth's life titled The Saint's Tragedy. And Elizabeth's tomb was long a shrine, until Philip, the Protestant landgrave of Hesse, removed her bones to an unknown place, not liking the Catholic veneration of the saint.

the sick. She even sold most of her jewels and a silver cradle in which she had been rocked as a baby.

Ludwig's stewards and treasurers met him on his return, accusing Elizabeth of bankrupting the treasury. Ludwig asked if she had lost any of his domains. The stewards had to admit that she had not. For her part, Elizabeth saw only that she had saved precious lives and possibly Ludwig's kingdom itself. "I gave God what was his and God has kept for us what was yours and mine," she told her husband. Ludwig appreciated her more than ever.

## Thrown Out Without a Penny

To fulfill a vow he had made, Ludwig joined Frederick II's crusade, leaving his lands in the charge of his brother, Henry Raspe IV. Elizabeth had a premonition that Ludwig would not return, and she dressed herself in widow's black. She was pregnant at the time, and after her child's birth in 1227, she learned that her husband had indeed died of fever. "The world is dead to me and all that was pleasant in the world," she cried, running through the castle and shrieking like one crazed.

Accounts differ as to what occurred after Ludwig's death. Some say that Henry seized power, throwing Elizabeth out of the castle. Other stories say that she left of her own accord. Claiming that she had ruined the treasury with her excessive concern for the poor, Henry cut off Elizabeth's allowance. In some accounts it is said that out of spite he forbade anyone in Eisenach, the nearby town, to assist her.

Alone and separated from her children, Elizabeth walked to Eisenach on a mid-winter evening. Despite her misery, she joined the Franciscans in singing a *Te Deum*. Because they feared Henry's reprisals, none of the townsfolk would open their doors to her. Even the convent turned her away. She was forced to spend the night in the courtyard of an inn among jars and baskets. She prayed that Christ would forgive those who had wronged her.

The next day some faithful ladies brought Elizabeth's children to her. She hugged the little ones and said to Herman, "May God so love me, I know not whither to turn, or where to rest your little bodies, though all the lordship of this town is yours, dear son."

Her loyal ladies promised to follow her wherever she went. They took refuge in the church that night. A poor priest brought them into his own home, and Elizabeth sold the few small jewels that she was wearing so that they could buy food. A few days later, a wealthy townsman gave them a corner in his house.

As she prayed, Elizabeth reflected on Christ's sufferings. Her Lord too had been out-cast and had borne cruel abuse. She asked Him to be with her, saying that she desired never to be parted from Him. Then the Lord showed Himself to her in a vision and said, "If you desire to be with me, I desire to be with you." We know nothing certain about her vision except that afterward she refused to wear crown jewels when entering the church to meditate on Christ, because she had seen Christ crowned with thorns and thought it unfitting for her to enter His presence wearing gems.

At the urging of Elizabeth's Aunt Mechthild, Egbert, bishop of Bamberg and Elizabeth's uncle, invited Elizabeth to come live in a house near his cathedral. On her way there, it is said that Elizabeth met the men who were returning from Italy with the coffin of her ill-fated husband. She nearly broke down, yet she told the Lord that even if she could have Ludwig back at the cost of no more than one of her hairs, "I would not call him back against Thy will."

## Reinstatement

The crusaders who had ridden forth with Ludwig spoke up for Elizabeth. They de-manded that her full domain be restored to her. For her part, she asked only for the res-toration of her son's rights and her dowry so that she might have enough money to carry out good deeds. In 1228 she gained her wish and Herman's inheritance was restored.

Elizabeth tried living in a castle that was hers by dowry and later in another that was hers by right of marriage, but Henry's ill will was so great that she finally built a simple cottage in Wehrda, near Marburg, and moved into it that same year. Pope Gregory IX sympathized with her and appointed Master Conrad of Marburg to be her protector and spiritual director.

It is likely that Elizabeth took some managing. Left to herself, she might well have used up her funds at once. She also would have begged door-to-door to raise support for her work. But Conrad did not allow these things to happen. In that regard, the require-ment of absolute obedience to one's religious superiors served a useful purpose.

Conrad was a sadistic man, however. He had been an inquisitor against heretics, and in his mind, the way to manage Elizabeth was to break her spirit. He set out to accom-plish that by dismissing her dearest friends. He excused the cruelty by saying that if he allowed them to remain with her, they would remind her of the past and turn her heart

Courtesy Christian History Institute archives

*Marburg Castle, another of Elizabeth's several homes*

away from her noble work. He set spies over her and went so far as to beat and slap her if she disobeyed his slightest command. He compelled her to accept the beatings and to flagellate herself. His methods did not succeed. Elizabeth compared herself to a water weed that bends flat in a flood and springs back up when the water level drops to normal.

Also in 1228, Elizabeth became a Franciscan tertiary (a layman penitent)—the first in the German Empire. She devoted the revenues from her dowry to building a hospital where she tended to the sick and spun wool. For extra income, she fished. Hers was one of Europe's first leprosariums. Many more followed and helped wipe out the disease in Europe.

## Death by Exhaustion

Elizabeth eventually overdid her exertions and died, probably of exhaustion, in 1231. She was not yet twenty-four years old. As she lay dying, she was heard singing in response to a bird who sat upon the wall. When the rooster crowed on her last day of life, she said, "It is now the time when He [Christ] rose from the grave and broke the doors of hell, and He will release me."

Her body was laid in the little chapel she had attached to her hospice. The blind, the lame, the demon-possessed and the lepers came to her funeral. A mere four years later, in 1235, the Roman Catholic Church named her a saint. Two hundred thousand people gathered for the occasion, convinced that Elizabeth had entered into a castle far grander than any of the five she had inhabited while she was alive on earth.

*Recommended reading: Nesta de Robeck,* St. Elizabeth of Hungary: A Study of Twenty-Four Years *(Milwaukee: Bruce Publishing, 1954).*

# QUEEN
## *of the*
# METHODISTS

Courtesy W.H. Daniels, *Illustrated History of Methodism* (New York: Hunt and Easton, 1890)

*H*ow can God make use of a woman who suffers from
ill health and mood swings? Although Lady Selina
Hastings, countess of Huntingdon, fit that description, she eventually became the "Queen of the Methodists."

Born in 1707, Selina was the second of three daughters and the coheiress of her father,
wealthy Washington Shirley, second Earl Ferrers. She married Theophilus Hastings at the
age of twenty-one, and her charitable deeds won her the nickname "Lady Bountiful."

By June of 1739, the birth of seven babies in rapid succession had left her with
gynecological injuries and frequent "colic." Some of
the best doctors in England had examined her, but
she seemed only to get worse. She feared for her life.
And in the dark recesses of her heart, she hugged a secret dread.

At thirty-two years of age, she was known for her
charitable works. She took seriously her responsibility to educate her servants in Christian living, distrib-
uting religious books among them. No one could
fault her church attendance. She read religious books
and contributed to orphanages, the Anglican Society
for Promoting Christian Knowledge and other charities, including a school for poor children, which she
took under her protection. And yet Selina feared for
her soul. It seemed to her that she always fell short of
the perfection God expected from His people. No
matter what she did, she felt that the distance between her and God was widening.

## Lady Selina Hastings

**Born:** August 24, 1707

**Education:** Poorly educated, despite her rank,
and never learned to
spell

**Married:** Theophilus Hastings on June 3, 1728

**Children:** Seven

**Died:** June 17, 1791, in
London, England

**Quote:** "Be no longer faithless, but believing."

*S*ome biographers suggest that Selina lived on the verge of hysteria. Yet she so consistently sponsored Methodism and shielded Methodists under her authority, sacrificing her entire fortune to their cause, that her life added up to something unusual.

*She trembled, believing that death was near. She hoped that she had been good enough to get into heaven. Even memories of her best actions did not relieve her apprehension. If anything, they made it worse, because even her best deeds seemed so insignificant. She felt like she would suffocate under the feeling that she was condemned! Was there no hope for her?*

*Then she remembered something her sister Margaret had once said. Margaret, despite ridicule, was attending the meetings of Benjamin Ingham, a Moravian who was closely associated with John and Charles Wesley, the Methodist leaders. What Margaret said was, "Since I have known and believed in the Lord Jesus Christ for salvation, I have been as happy as an angel." The words were like a foreign language to Selina, although she had to admit that Margaret did seem happier than she had been before. What did her words mean?*

*As Selina pondered Margaret's words, the truth became clear to her. She could expect pardon from God for her bad attitudes and raging temper not because of any good thing she had done but only because Jesus offered it as a free gift. "I believe!" she cried.*

## Turning Point

July of 1739 marked a turning point in Selina's religious life. She was filled with enthusiasm for the Methodist movement and supported it for the rest of her life. Throughout England, the Methodists were preaching in fields and rousing common people to a new level of faith. At once Selina sent one of her own servants, David Taylor, to preach in the fields. She read religious books to her workers with renewed fervor and pleaded with them to become spiritually minded. To one worker she said, "Thomas, I fear you never pray, or look to Christ to salvation."

"Your ladyship is mistaken," replied Thomas. "I heard what passed between you and James at the garden wall, and the word you meant for him took effect on me."

"How did you hear it?" she asked.

"Through a hole in the wall, and I shall never forget the impression I received."

Selina also wrote letters to her friends—England's duchesses and leading ladies—telling them that knowing Christ as a companion would transform their lives. She coaxed several to attend chapel with her, but they did not become converted as she hoped. She hired zealous chaplains and, whenever she took a summer holiday, brought them along and had them preach to crowds at every stop. The result was many conversions for the Methodists.

## Shifting Sands

In spite of her new enthusiasm, Selina was not happy. Her aims shifted with her moods. She abruptly abandoned a school that she had taken under her protection, leaving its masters jobless and the bewildered children to find other arrangements. She broke her relationship with Benjamin Ingham when he married her sister, Margaret, in 1741, because the marriage cut Selina's daughter, Elizabeth, out of an inheritance and because the couple had lived together before they were married.

Courtesy Christian History Institute archives

*Charles Wesley*

Increasingly Selina turned to the Wesleys for guidance. In 1741 she invited John and Charles for a visit to her estate at Donington. She became their fervent admirer and adopted John Wesley's doctrine of perfection, saying that it was a doctrine that she hoped to live and die by. At the same time, she played one brother against the other, hinting in letters that one or the other liked her better, complaining to Charles about John's faults and vice versa, and pestered them with desperate letters. "No soul can conceive the darkness, perplexity, misery I have constantly surrounding me," she wrote.

The death of her mother and two of her children, quarrels with her sisters over a will and the failure of the Jacobite rebellion in Scotland between 1745 and 1746 contributed to that darkness and misery. Selina had hoped the Jacobites would succeed for moral reasons. She considered the court of King George II to be dreadfully corrupt and thought that the descendants of King James II would uplift the monarchy. The year after the Jacobite rebellion, Selina's husband died, adding to her grief.

Her friendships with John and Charles cooled as she drew closer to another Methodist, the Calvinist George Whitefield. She embraced his interpretation of the doctrine of predestination, which emphasized God's sovereign choice in salvation and opposed the Wesleyan teaching that emphasized man's role in deciding the issue. Eventually the Methodists split over this very issue. Selina tried to reconcile the two sides in 1749, but

*W*hat blessed ef-
fects does the
love of God produce in the
hearts of those who abide
in him. How solid is the
peace, and how divine the
joy that springs from an
assurance that we are
united to the Savior by a
living faith. . . . I am
deeply sensible that daily,
hourly, and momentarily
I stand in need of sprin-
kling of my Savior's blood.
—Lady Selina
Hastings to
Charles Wesley

she finally broke with the Wesleys. She had found that she could not live up to John's doctrine of perfection and openly attacked it. She denounced John as "a papist unmasked, a heretic and an apostate."

## Devoted to a Cause

In spite of her changing doctrine and shift in allegiance from Wesley to Whitefield, Selina used her rank to protect the Methodists. She remained a devoted supporter of the Methodist movement to the end of her life.

Methodists needed all the support they could get. They were often badly abused, even by the very authorities who should have protected them. Riots and beatings were common when Methodist preachers came to town. At other times, legal harassment was employed.

Sir Watkins Wynn, an enemy of revivalists, fined men who were caught listening to the preaching of Howel Harris, a Welsh evangelist. The fines were between five and twenty shillings each—large sums in those days. Selina immediately approached the governing authorities, invoking the Toleration Act, and Sir Wynn was forced to refund the fines.

The people of the town of Brighton could also testify to Selina's devotion. When its poor needed a place to worship, Selina, who had no money to give, sold her jewels to build them a chapel. It was one of more than sixty chapels across England whose construction she funded.

Selina sought to be guided by faith. One man called on her to scold her for trying to open another chapel in London when she did not have the money to finish projects she had already started. She insisted on pushing ahead with the project. While they talked, the mail came. In one letter was this note: "An individual who has heard of Lady Huntingdon's exertions to spread the gospel, requests her acceptance of the enclosed draft." Tears of joy rolled down Selina's cheeks. Enclosed was £500, the sum that was needed to build the chapel in London. "Here," she said to the man. "Take it and pay for the chapel; and be no longer faithless but believing."

Lady Selina's chapels were built in the belief that, as a peeress, she had the right to employ any number of chaplains. By hiring Methodists, she spread over them her coat of authority. This interpretation of the law was challenged by leaders of the Church of England, and the Consistorial Court of London ruled against Selina in 1779. That ruling labeled her chaplains dissenters under the law and their chapels dissenting places of worship. Selina and her associates were forced to register under the Toleration Act.

For years Selina had remained loyal to the Church of England, viewing Methodism as simply a reform movement within the established Church. Now she wrote, "I am to be cast out of the church now only for doing what I have been doing these forty years—speaking and living for Jesus Christ."

Courtesy Christian History Institute archives

*Officials ignore an attack on Methodists in Cork.*

## Brush of Death

Always weak, Selina felt the brush of death against her cheek several times, and when she was eighty-three, death again approached. When she came from her chamber one morning, her friends saw an unusual light upon her countenance. "The Lord hath been present with my spirit this morning in a remarkable manner; what he means to convey to my mind I know not; it may be my approaching departure: my soul is filled with glory—I am as in the element of heaven itself." A few days later, one of her blood vessels ruptured, and she never recovered. Hours before her death she whispered, "I shall go to my father tonight." She died on June 17, 1791.

When Selina's will was read, it was discovered that she had left inadequate provision for carrying on the work that she had started. Her schools and chapels were not endowed, and serious debts were due.

People's feelings about Selina were mixed. Some saw her as quarrelsome, erratic and despotic. Her own children rejected her faith—she laid all but one of them in the grave unconverted, and that one was saved by a deathbed repentance whose sincerity she doubted. And yet hymn writer Augustus Toplady called Selina "the most precious saint of God" he ever knew, and Philip Doddridge, a noble-minded clergyman and author of the influential *Rise and Progress of Religion in the Soul*, wrote to his wife,

She is quite a mother to the poor; she visits them and prays with them in sickness, and they leave their children to her for a legacy when they die and she takes care of them. I was really astonished at the traces of religion which I discovered in her . . . and cannot but glorify God for them. More cheerfulness I never saw mingled with so much devotion.

Few women have had so unique an opportunity to defend a reform movement within the Church and used it so willingly. Thousands benefited from Selina's life. Her poor health and emotional instability may have kept her from even greater achievements, but God saw fit to uniquely use her all the same.

*Recommended reading: Edwin Welch,* Spiritual Pilgrim: A Reassessment of the Life of the Countess of Huntingdon *(Cardiff: University of Wales, 1995).*

# "GOD, HELP ME
## *to*
# HELP THEM"

*R*ose Hawthorne Lathrop listened aghast as Rev. Alfred Young told the story of a young seamstress, a sensitive and cultured woman, who took ill of cancer. Terrified of the disease, the seamstress' landlady threw her out of her room. A private hospital sent the seamstress to a city hospital, where she was packed off to a poorhouse on Blackwell Island. Alone and friendless, thrown among criminals, the seamstress died in despair. Her life savings had been eaten up in a hopeless search for a cure, and her body was dumped into a pauper's grave.

As bad as it is to contract cancer today, it was worse in the 1800s. People feared the disease like we fear leprosy or ebola. A person could be thrown out of his apartment with nowhere to go if he were dying of cancer, and this was exactly what had happened to one hard-working, gentle seamstress.

Rose was told that there was little that could be done once a person was pronounced incurable. Hospitals existed to cure people, not to house them through months or years of agonizing decline. And so they turned cancer patients out at the very moment when their need was the greatest. When the dying wanted only compassion and a place to ease their pain and hide their disfigurement, they were pushed out to die among criminals and strangers, their misery made worse by the loss of privacy and the smells and moans of fellow sufferers.

## Rose Lathrop

**Born:** May 20, 1851, in Lenox, MA

**Education:** Educated at home and by childhood travels

**Married:** George Lathrop in 1871

**Children:** One son, who died in infancy

**Died:** July 9, 1926, in Hawthorne, NY

**Quote:** "God, help me to help them."

## A Flood of Tears

Back in her room, Rose sat down to think. Her marriage to George Lathrop was rocky because George had turned to alcohol, but that no longer

113

*Nathaniel Haw-thorne, Rose's fa-ther, was the author of* The Scarlett Letter. *Her mother, Sophia Peabody, came from a family that was reputed to have roots that went back to Queen Boadicea of England. Visitors called young Rose "The Rose of all the Haw-thornes" because of her beauty and charm. Her philosophy was simple: "If time made any alterations in so vital a matter as the best methods of charity, Christ would have told us so. . . . He has not said a word to contradict His first teaching, simple, direct, unavoidable, leading to personal sacrifice and immediate Holy love."*

seemed like the ultimate tragedy that it once had. There were worse fates in life—like that of the seamstress.

Rose had not been particularly aware of cancer until she had visited her dying friend, the poet Emma Lazarus. Emma was the author of the words on the Statue of Liberty, "Give me your tired, your poor, your huddled masses. . . ." The end of her life had been eased by all the comforts that money could buy and the love of a caring family, and yet pain had tightened her lips and an unpleasant odor had hung over her room. *What must cancer be like for the poor, who have no room, no comforts, no money?* thought Rose.

Having recently embraced the Catholic faith (the beauties of Catholic religious art had drawn Rose away from her parents' Unitarianism to the Catholic Church), Rose knew that Christ would expect her to do something about the tragedy of cancer. She fell to her knees, tears flowing from beneath her eyelids, and prayed, "God, help me to help them."

A plan formed in her mind. She would open a clinic for victims of incurable cancer. She would even take in a few homeless patients—women utterly without resources and friends. Rose communicated her vision to Josephine Lazarus, sister of the dead poet. Josephine tried to dissuade Rose. After Emma's death, she said, she had opened a small hospital herself. Even with quality equipment, top pay and short hours, nurses could not be kept on staff and the project had failed. Josephine predicted disaster should Rose attempt to open a hospital. All the same, she sent a gift of money to be applied toward the work.

However, Rose realized that something more than money was needed, and that something was faith. Rose offered herself, in faith, to tackle the task.

## A Rose Among Thorns

Friends and acquaintances were astonished at Rose's decision. "What made you choose such a dirty occupation?" one asked.

It was a good question. Well-born and highly cultured, Rose moved in the highest literary and artistic circles of New England and New York. Her stories appeared in the *Atlantic Monthly* and *St. Nicholas* magazine, and she had published a volume of poems titled *Along the Shore*. Yet, there she was, throwing away her literary future and taking a small house in the slums in which to change filthy, smelly bandages.

Many years later, Rose answered the question in an account that appeared in the *New York Times*. She said that she had been brought up by compassionate parents who, by their example, taught her to help sufferers. She especially remembered the day when her father, a famous author, overcame his natural repugnance for de-

Courtesy the Dominican Sisters of Hawthorne

*Alice Huber*

formity and picked up and stroked a half-witted, sore-covered child who was pleading for affection. The death of Emma Lazarus, who was so similar to Rose in station and interests, had also affected her, but it was the despairing death of the seamstress that had forced her into action.

Rose's belief that one must die to one's own interests in order to live for Christ also played its part in her choice. Her brother, Julian, wrote, "Nothing less than the extreme would satisfy her thirst for self-sacrifice. Whatever was most abhorrent to the instincts of the flesh, that she must embrace; whatsoever was most hopeless or forlorn in human fate, that must she love and assuage."

## Charity of Heart and Hands

Rose was practical. She knew nothing about bandaging wounds and nothing about treating cancer, so in 1896 she volunteered for three months at a hospital where she could learn the skills she needed. As her fingers plucked at the gauze to lift off her first bandage, she found a face that had been eaten away by cancer. It took all of her resolution to go through with her task.

*I was storm-tossed with dismay in the first few months of initiation, when beginning my work for the few sick poor on the East Side of New York, whom I could manage to attend to; but after a time sailed into a gentle sea, where I gazed calmly towards the peace of God's mercy, the glowing but unchanging horizon of presiding heaven, of which the circle is always about us, so lovingly.*
                *—Rose Lathrop*

Mustering her courage, she overcame her horror and in a few weeks was able to do the job without shrinking back. At about that same time she acquired a small home that was situated between two horse stables in New York's east-side slums. Her first live-in patient was the same Irish woman whose face she had treated in the hospital. Mrs. Watson was a prankster, and as long as she was able to, she devoted herself to helping Rose. She often filled the house with laughter, but her mind began to fail from the morphine, pain and blindness.

It turned out that Mrs. Watson had a family, but they imposed on Rose by refusing to house Mrs. Watson and care for her themselves. A particularly troublesome grandson came to stay in the house as well, but he behaved so badly with acts of arson and vandalism that he threatened to undo the mission. Rose sent the boy away, but Mrs. Watson never smiled after that and Rose found herself out of patience with the woman. The experience showed her a picture of her own heart:

> I resented her [Mrs. Watson] having affectionate patience with her low, unfilial children, and her want of that uprightness which I preferred, and her half-insane complaints when we did our best. She perceived this by my brief, cold answers when she was putting me to the test, and I daily grieved over my want of magnanimity! and I won tender words from her once more only to resent her unreasonable sallies again. I proved a thousand times that charitable acts and laborious services are no better than tares when the spirit does not speak to the soul we serve in full and humble accord. As I sat by her simple black coffin in our shanty room, before taking her to our lot for burial, I had no thought for anything but the fact that I was a poor friend to the poor, a heartless judge of a kinder heart than my own, and a darker failure in better light than the woman who had often prayed for me, and never injured me in the least.

Rose determined anew to love deeply those she treated in her home. Even amid the depressing scene of patients dying of incurable cancer, she would burst into infectious laughter over anything humorous and would thus cheer her patients as well as herself.

## Sacrifice and Hardships

To educate the public about the needs of cancer victims, Rose issued a little magazine, beginning in 1901, called *Christ's Poor*, which was filled with stories of cancer patients.

Late in 1897, one reader of *Christ's Poor*, Alice Huber, came to visit Rose. She later wrote,

Courtesy the Dominican Sisters of Hawthorne

*Rosary Hill in 2000*

> I found Water Street after some difficulty, but when I came to 668 I hesitated going in; it was a dilapidated frame building, there was no bell, and the door leading into the hall was open. . . . A fair, bright faced woman (who was bandaging up an old woman's leg) rose from her work and came forward to meet me. . . . I sat down on a green sofa, the only comfortable thing in the room, and glanced about; everything was clean, but as crowded, poor and simple as could be; Mrs. Lathrop was beautiful and youthful looking, with a mass of rich auburn hair; she wore a nurse's dress and her manner of dealing with the old women was cheerful and simple.

Though she was repulsed by the women whom Rose tended and distressed by the neighborhood, Alice still could not leave without offering to help. She volunteered to come one afternoon a week. The following Tuesday, she came as she had promised.

> I must say that I felt intense disgust that first time, but Mrs. Lathrop seemed so cheerful and happy, and looked so pleadingly at me as I was leaving that I said I could come again. After a while I came two afternoons of each week, and in a few months' time resolved to leave the world and come live with Mrs. Lathrop. It was only then that I began to realize the sacrifice and hardships of her life; it was work early and late, sometimes far into the night; we were surrounded for the most part by a low class of people; we had no time for reading, I could not even write a letter . . . the patients groaned, the women in the kitchen rattled pots and pans, and the people in the neighborhood never seemed to go to bed. . . . We were at that time extremely poor—boxes served as chairs, and we ate in the kitchen with the untidy women and some of the patients.

Alice was the first of many who were drawn into Rose's work.

## A Rose by Any Other Name Is a Rose the Same

On December 8, 1900, three years after Alice's first visit, she and Rose Lathrop took vows in a Catholic order. They established The Dominican Congregation of St. Rose of Lima (Servants of Relief for Incurable Cancer). Rose took the name Sister Alphonsa, and Alice took the name Sister Rose.

Their work expanded. In 1901, Rose took up residence at Rosary Hill in Hawthorne, New York, which became the mother home for her cancer work. By Rose's death in 1926, she had ministered to thousands of cancer patients, and during her thirty years of cancer work, she had drawn hundreds of helpers to the task. As a result of her prayers and appeals, hospitals were built for cancer patients, in part through the voluntary contributions of the men and women who toiled beside her.

Rose Lathrop's funeral was preached by the Very Reverend James A. Walsh, a friend of many years. He stated,

> She loved all with a heart full to overflowing, and she loved God with her whole mind. . . . I do not exaggerate when I say that she could have taken her place in the chronicles of American literature, but she sought higher things. Her mind flew to God; she gave it to Him; she diverted it to His purposes, and He accepted it, and she loved Him with her whole mind.

Though she is merely a footnote in the history of literature, Rose stands as a giant of charity.

*Recommended reading: Sister M. Joseph, O.P.* Out of Many Hearts: Mother M. Alphonsa Lathrop and Her Work *(Hawthorne, NY: Servants of Relief for Incurable Cancer, 1965).*

# DIAMOND-DUST SOCIALITE

Courtesy Delores T. Burger, *Women Who Changed the Heart of the City* (Grand Rapids, MI: Kregel Publications, 1997)

*T*he Door of Hope home needed a new piano. Emma Whittemore brought the girls together to pray for one, but told them to say nothing about it to anyone outside of the home. Almost immediately, someone sent them a wind-up music box, and one of the girls wondered if God had misunderstood their prayer. Emma assured her that God had not, and before long God also provided them with a beautiful piano.

Later, they needed a piano stool. Emma again led the girls in prayer, and they had hardly gotten up from their knees when there was a knock at the door. Opening the door, they found a piano stool on the steps. They never found out who had left it there. Through her example, Emma demonstrated a life of prayer to the girls whom she had rescued from the streets.

## Emma Whittemore

**Born:** May 20, 1850
**Education:** Unknown
**Married:** Sidney Whittemore on September 11, 1871
**Children:** One
**Died:** September 30, 1931
**Quote:** *"We arose with a holy determination, born of God himself, to henceforth live for His glory and praise."*

## Truly Transformed

Money, servants, dinners, parties, balls—Emma had it all. Born in 1850, she was the daughter of a notable lawyer and the granddaughter of one of New York's wealthiest surgeons. She married a prominent businessman, Sidney Whittemore, and together they moved among the elite of New York. Her wealth allowed her to clothe herself in dresses that glittered with diamond dust. As far as the Whittemores were concerned, there was nothing they lacked.

One afternoon in 1875, Emma's friend Miss Kelly persuaded Emma to come hear an English

*Betrayed and then cruelly deserted [a pitiful fifteen-year-old] . . . would have been left utterly friendless, unwilling to relinquish her baby. After a brief conversation, I informed her that we had not thought of taking children. Before I could explain any further, big tears flowed down her face as she said: "Oh, I'd rather walk the streets and starve with my baby in my arms than to have a place to stay and give him up. Every place I've been refuses to take me because I have a baby, but I just won't give him up. I love him too much to let him go."*

*I concluded it was no time for talking, so I simply replied: "Well, dear, let us kneel together and ask what the Lord wants us to do."*

*(cont'd on next page)*

evangelist, Henry Varley, speak at the YMCA. In one of those coincidences that signal the hand of God at work, Sidney also went independently to the meeting. "My husband had been ignorant of the fact that I was in the building, and I had not the slightest thought that he would be present," wrote Emma. Both of them were stirred by the message and at the end of the service went down to the mourner's bench, where they made "firm resolutions to live a different life."

Miss Kelly called on Emma again and asked if Emma would go with her to Water Street to see Jerry McAuley, an ex-convict and a reformed drunkard who had opened a mission in a rough area of New York City. Sidney was reluctant to allow his wife to visit the dance hall where McAuley preached, but just this once, he said, she could go, and he would escort her.

"Never can that night be erased from my memory," wrote Emma. "From the time we got off the car at Roosevelt Street, each step opened up some new horror." She heard curses and witnessed quarreling, fighting, police abuse and women being dragged off to the police station.

The smells in the dance hall were vile, for it was crowded with "sin-bedraggled people." McAuley's gruff voice hollered at them to have a seat in the front. "We had not been accustomed to that kind of treatment," said Emma. Sidney spoke condescending words about the poor people who were gathered in the hall.

"As the meeting progressed, however, God got such possession of him and later on myself also that we were both held in painful silence as we were convicted of our useless lives. We no longer felt superior to the 'poor creatures' around us but actually hung our heads in shame."

McAuley preached, people sang and the meeting was thrown open for testimonies. Badly dressed slum tenants leapt up, praising the Lord that they were daily kept from sin amid terrible temptations. Emma and Sidney saw "that these people were truly transformed and possessed the genuine thing and not the veneer that characterized some professed Christians in the social circle that had engrossed our time and thought." Overcome by emotion, Sidney stood and requested prayer, a tear trickling through the fingers in which he hid his face. He was such "a stiff Presbyterian and had been so very conventional" that Emma was astonished.

"I thought he had never appeared nobler or braver in my eyes. I could not let him stand alone. Where he would go, I would go." So she rose and stood beside him. Jerry called them to kneel with the others at the mourner's bench. A motley group surrounded them, including "a drunkard, a thief and a tramp on my husband's side, and on my side one or two poor women." With the drunkard they prayed, "God be merciful to me a sinner—for Jesus' sake." The Spirit of God witnessed to their spirits that their prayer was heard.

"We arose with a holy determination, born of God himself, to hence-forth live for his glory and praise. From that night I date the giving up of a worldly life," wrote Emma. Eager to see souls won to Christ, Emma and Sidney began to regularly haunt the dance hall—the place they had said they would visit only "this once." There Emma learned practical methods of showing love and was taught to give her testimony.

*. . . With my arm around the trembling shoulders I could somehow better appreciate the depths of the motherly love that was in her heart even though she was only a child herself. . . . I offered fervent prayer in her behalf and before arising from our knees, the matter was settled. I pressed a kiss on her cheek as I said, "Hannah, dear child, I'll take you both. You may bring your baby." Throwing her arms around my neck and weeping with joy, the child-mother exclaimed, "Oh, then I can, I can have my baby, my own dear little baby!"*

—Emma Whittemore

## Miracle Before Miracles

That Emma was able to visit Water Street at all was a miracle in itself. Years earlier she had broken one of her lower vertebrae in a fall, and for twelve years she had lived in severe pain, at times bedridden. When her suffering was at its peak, she had to be car-

*In light of her accomplishments, it is hard to believe that Emma Whittemore was once such a timid person that she hardly dared to ask for a spool of thread if she had dropped it. After she founded Door of Hope, she spoke with a power that astonished veteran evangelists.*

ried up and down stairs. Her condition became so bad that she declared she would "rather die than live."

In 1884 Dr. A.B. Simpson, soon to become the founder of The Christian and Missionary Alliance, was proclaiming healing and sanctification in New York City. Emma became interested enough to hear him speak, but she was so skeptical that she walked out of the first meeting. Her own pastor tried to keep her from believing that there was any truth to divine healing, and for a time she herself ridiculed the notion. Yet she could not keep herself from going back to Simpson's church, listening to testimonies and speaking with the preacher himself.

Finally, she decided to settle the matter to her own satisfaction. For four days she shut herself away with her Bible. At the close of the fourth day, alone in her room, she committed her body to God for healing. "He enabled me to claim healing upon the authority of His Word," she said. She waited for His promise to come to pass.

When her little son assured her that God would do what He said He would, she got off her bed, determined to believe God for complete deliverance from her pain. The very next evening, as she prepared for bed, she found herself in a position that had always caused her agony for the last twelve years. This time she felt only a bruised sensation. In joy, she cried aloud, "O Lord, I'm healed, I'm healed."

## "Anything but That!"

One evening Emma spent some time "alone with God, earnestly inquiring of Him" what she was to do now that she was healed. "Suddenly the girls on the street came to my mind so forcibly that it was not difficult to almost imagine I could hear the tramp of numberless feet going straight to damnation." But the thought of working with those wayward women horrified her. "Oh, anything but that!" she pleaded.

A deep hush of shame came upon her heart, "and in the stillness which followed, He caused me to realize that there was in my heart a serious lack of love." If she disobeyed, she would lose a great chance to serve God and be blessed. She sensed that God was promising her that He would make provision for her to meet every need. She agreed to work with the desperately needy women and began to do so that very evening.

"The horrors we witnessed nearly overpowered us. Often after such nights of tramping the streets, have I dropped upon my knees as I reached home and in tears cried out, 'Oh, Lord, I cannot, I cannot see these fearful sights again! It simply breaks my heart.' " In response to her prayer, she always received more love with which she could go on.

## Door of Hope

If girls were to be rescued, homes were needed to house them. On October 25, 1890, "Mother" Whittemore, as she came to be called, opened the first Door of Hope ministry in a house belonging to A.B. Simpson. Emma vowed that she would never go through normal channels to raise funds,

Courtesy R.M. Offord, *Jerry McAuley: An Apostle to the Lost* (American Tract Society, 1907)

*Jerry McAuley*

but rather she would tell every need directly to God. She did not even mention her home's needs to her own husband.

Only once did she hint of a need, and though the money was immediately and generously supplied, afterward the funds dried up. She apologized to God, and the funds came again. Needless to say, that was the last time she ever even hinted at a need. Nevertheless, unsolicited donations came at just the right moment, time after time, to meet the needs of Door of Hope and prove that God's hand was driving the work.

Within 4 years, Door of Hope had helped 325 girls. Emma's first concern was to bring them to know the power of Christ in their lives as she had experienced it in hers. Welfare agencies might bring girls out of the dens of vice, she said, "but only Jesus can get the vice out of the girls." Her second aim was to make the girls active participants in the mission's efforts to convert others. Some had surprising success, but none more so than Delia Loughlin, formerly a violent "underworld" figure, who led 100 of her earlier associates to become Christians. Door of Hope eventually went international. By Emma's death in 1931, there were ninety-seven such homes in the United States, Canada, Great Britain, Germany, Africa, Japan and China.

Emma proved through her own example what great things a woman can accomplish when Christ becomes her supreme love.

*Recommended reading: Emma M. Whittemore,* Records of Modern Miracles, *edited by F.A. Robinson (Toronto, Ontario: Missions of Biblical Education, 1947).*

# Part 6
## Handicap? What Handicap?

*They were not
deterred by old age,
youth or defect.*

# Too Young *to* Serve?

*T*hey gathered together for the drawing of lots. The time had come to select a leader, a "chief eldress" for the women in the bustling community of Moravians at Herrnhut (in what is now eastern Germany). Four names were put on slips of paper. One was Anna Nitschmann. Only fourteen years old, she had already demonstrated leadership among the single women.

The girl must have tried hard to appear calm as the choice was announced. It was Anna. Was it a suppressed smile or a look of fright that crossed her face as her name was read? She probably noticed some scowls of consternation among the others. The drawing of lots was supposed to discern the leading of God—but she was so young. In this case, had there been a mistake?

## Anna Nitschmann

**Born:** 1715

**Education:** Attended schools in Moravia and Herrnhut

**Married:** Count von Zinzendorf in June of 1757

**Children:** None

**Died:** 1760 at Herrnhut

**Quote:** "Jesus, Thou fain would'st have us be in all things more conformed to Thee."

## Spiritual Awakening

The Moravians were one of the most interesting groups in the history of Christianity. Spiritual heirs of the Bohemian martyr Jan Hus, they suffered religious persecution for generations until a remnant of them found refuge at Count Zinzendorf's estate in 1722. There they built a town called Herrnhut, and a growing, thriving community developed.

While still in Moravia, Anna Nitschmann's father and older brother had been jailed for their Christian faith. They managed to escape to Herrnhut in 1725, and there they became actively involved in the Moravian community.

By 1727 dissensions had sprung up within the community. Various feuds and grudges were disrupting the happy place. Concerned leaders prayed

127

*It was said of Anna that "when she spoke or prayed or sang, all hearts stood open to her."*

earnestly about the developing problems, and after a communion service on August 13, 1727, an unusual spiritual awakening swept across the people there.

The whole community sensed that they needed to turn from their pettiness and pursue God's calling. Those with bad attitudes repented, relationships were restored and an around-the-clock prayer meeting was begun, with teams taking one hour at a time. (This prayer meeting would continue for over 100 years!)

One of those who were deeply affected by the spiritual awakening was Anna Nitschmann, who was then just twelve years old. She dedicated her life to the Lord's service and immediately began organizing the young women of the community into a kind of club for worship and ministry. It was this activity that caught the eye of community leaders and made them nominate her for the position of chief eldress.

## God's Choice

In a way, Anna's sudden stature in the community was surprising. She'd been a bit rebellious shortly after her family escaped to Herrnhut. She seemed to lose interest in religious things, and the severe turmoil that the community was experiencing at the time didn't help much. When anyone in the community would press for Anna's conversion, she would snap, "First get converted yourself, and then talk to me." It was the awakening of August 1727 that turned her around.

Count Zinzendorf, the leader of the Moravian movement, strongly advised Anna to refuse the appointment to the position of chief eldress, but the young peasant girl respectfully reminded the nobleman that she was accepting the appointment as from the Lord. Just as the surprising choice of the shepherd boy, David, proved decisive for Israel, so the choice of young Anna would prove decisive for the Moravians.

Six weeks after the election, Anna led eighteen of the "single sisters" to devote themselves so thoroughly to Christ that even marriage would take second place. This commitment was a major one, signaling a serious desire to serve the Lord. This "single sisters" group would grow over the following decades, providing a stream of courageous missionaries.

Later, in 1736, Anna became part of the "Pilgrim congregation," a group of spiritual storm troopers who were ready to go anywhere to spread the name of Christ. Her mission travels took her to numerous countries, even to America, where she helped in the founding of Bethlehem and Nazareth, Pennsylvania, in the early 1740s and ministered effectively among various Indian groups. In an era when women were not looked upon as hymn writers, Anna wrote more than thirty hymns that were published in the Moravians' German hymnal.

Courtesy the Comenius Foundation

*Herrnhut*

Anna twice refused offers of marriage, but one year after Count Zinzendorf's wife died, he asked Anna to marry him and she agreed. She was a commoner and he a noble, but within the Herrnhut community, all were equals. Anna, then forty-one, had long since proven her total Christian commitment. They were married in June of 1757.

By the time of Anna Nitschmann's death in 1760, the Moravians had sent out 226 missionaries and baptized more than 3,000 converts. That was only thirty-eight years since the founding of the Herrnhut community and only twenty-eight years since they had sent their first missionaries out into the world. Among those deeply influenced by the Moravians were John and Charles Wesley.

To the early Moravians, Anna was known as the *Selige Juengerin*, the "Blessed Woman Disciple." By example she demolished doubts about what a young person—or a woman—could do in the service of Christ.

*Recommended reading: Grethe Goodwin,* Anna Nitschmann, 1715-1760: Founder of the Moravian Single Sisters Choir *(Bethlehem, PA: Oaks Press, 1985).*

# QUEEN *of* AMERICAN HYMN WRITERS

*O*ne day, while engaged in prison ministry, Fanny Crosby heard a prisoner cry out, asking the Lord not to pass him by. The plea haunted Fanny's memory, and she went home and wrote the well-known hymn "Pass Me Not, O Gentle Savior." A few days later, she passed out in the same prison, overcome by emotion when several prisoners gave their lives to Christ after hearing her new hymn sung.

## Fanny Crosby

**Born:** March 24, 1820, in Putnam County, NY

**Education:** Attended the Institute for the Blind in NY

**Married:** Alexander van Alstine on March 5, 1858

**Children:** One daughter named Frances, who died in infancy

**Died:** February 12, 1915, in Bridgeport, CT

**Quote:** *"How in the world could I have lived such a helpful life as I have lived had I not been blind?"*

## Blinded by a Quack

Francis Jane Crosby was born into a family of strong Puritan ancestry in New York on March 24, 1820. As a baby, she contracted an eye infection, which a quack doctor treated by placing hot poultices on her inflamed eyelids. The infection cleared up, but scars formed on her eyes, and the baby girl became blind for life. A few months later, Fanny's father grew ill and died. Mercy Crosby, widowed at twenty-one, hired herself out as a maid while Grandmother Eunice Crosby took care of little Fanny.

Grandmother Eunice took the education of her granddaughter upon herself and became the girl's eyes, vividly describing the physical world to Fanny. Eunice's careful teaching helped develop Fanny's

Courtesy Allan Sutherland, *Famous Hymns of the World, Their Origin and Their Romance* (New York: Frederick A. Stokes Company, 1906)

*W.H. Doane asked Fanny to write him a hymn in forty minutes. The result was "Safe in the Arms of Jesus."*

descriptive abilities, and she also nurtured Fanny's soul. She read and carefully explained the Bible to the little girl, always emphasizing the importance of prayer. When Fanny became depressed because she couldn't learn as other children did, Eunice taught her to pray to God for knowledge. Despite Eunice's influence, it was not until 1850, when she was thirty years old, that Fanny truly yielded her heart to Christ at a camp meeting.

A landlady of the Crosbys also had an important role in Fanny's development. Mrs. Hawley helped Fanny memorize the Bible, and the young girl sometimes learned five chapters a week. She knew the Pentateuch, the Gospels, Proverbs, the Song of Solomon and many of the psalms by heart. She developed a memory that amazed her friends, but Fanny believed that she was no different from others. Her blindness had simply forced her to develop her memory and her powers of concentration more.

Fanny did not look on her blindness as a terrible thing. Even at eight years old she composed this little verse:

> Oh, what a happy child I am,
> Although I cannot see!
> I am resolved that in this world
> Contented I will be!
> How many blessings I enjoy
> That other people don't!
> So weep or sigh because I'm blind,
> I cannot—nor I won't.

## A Blind Girl's Cheerful Outlook

Blindness never produced self-pity in Fanny. In her adult years she would say, "It was the best thing that could have happened to me," or "How in the world could I have lived such a helpful life as I have lived had I not been blind?"

In 1834 Fanny learned of the New York Institute for the Blind and knew that the school was the answer to her prayer for an education. She entered the school when she was twelve years old and upon graduating went on to teach there for twenty-three years. She became somewhat of a celebrity at the school and was called upon to write poems for almost every conceivable occasion.

On March 5, 1858, Fanny married Alexander van Alstine, a former pupil at the Institute. He was a musician who was considered one of the finest organists in the New York area. Fanny herself was an excellent harpist, played the piano and had a lovely soprano voice. Even as an elderly woman (she lived to be ninety-five) Fanny would sit at the piano and play everything from classical works to hymns to ragtime music. Sometimes she even played old hymns in a jazzed-up style.

## Making Much Music

After her marriage to Alexander, Fanny left the Institute. In January of 1864 she had a vision in which the Lord told her that He had work for her to do, and she heard the music of heaven. At about that same time her pastor arranged for Fanny to meet William B. Bradbury.

Bradbury, a composer, organist, music publisher and instrument maker, was composing a new kind of flowing music that was delightful to common listeners and churchgoers but scorned by highbrow critics. A Bradbury tune that is known to almost everyone today is "Jesus Loves Me."

The two met on February 2, 1864, and immediately hit it off, though not many of their musical combinations are remembered. It was at Bradbury's establishment that Fanny met William H. Doane in November of 1867. Doane was delighted to connect with her, for he too had been looking for a writer. Among the songs he wrote with Fanny were "I Am Thine, O Lord" and "Pass Me Not, O Gentle Savior."

In the 1860s Fanny came to an agreement with the publishers Bigelow and Main to write three hymns a week for use in their Sunday school publications. Sometimes she wrote six or

*Much of Fanny Crosby's influence on others was through her hymn writing. William Bradbury, composer, organist, music publisher and instrument maker, was looking for quality Christian verse to set to his music. When Fanny set words to an "impossible" piece of music, Bradbury took her on. That was the start of her hymn ministry, for Bradbury introduced her to W.H. Doane, with whom she wrote her most memorable songs.*

*When my life-work is ended and I cross the swelling tide,/ When the bright and glorious morning I shall see,/ I shall know my Redeemer when I reach the other side,/ And His smile will be the first to welcome me.*
*Chorus:*
*I shall know Him, I shall know Him,/ And redeemed by His side I shall stand!/ I shall know Him, I shall know Him/ By the print of the nails in His hand.*

*—Fanny Crosby*

seven hymns a day. She was usually paid only a dollar or two for each poem. Those who composed the tunes usually kept the rights to the entire hymn.

Though Fanny could write complex poetry as well as improvise music of classical structure, her hymns were aimed at bringing the message of the gospel to people who would not listen to preaching. Whenever she wrote a hymn, she prayed that God would use it to lead many souls to Him.

## Music for the Masses

In her own day, the evangelistic team of Dwight L. Moody and Ira D. Sankey effectively brought Fanny Crosby's hymns to the masses. Today several of these songs continue to draw souls to their Savior for both salvation and comfort: "Blessed Assurance," "All the Way My Savior Leads Me," "To God Be the Glory," "Pass Me Not, O Gentle Savior," "Safe in the Arms of Jesus," "Rescue the Perishing," "Jesus, Keep Me Near the Cross," "I Am Thine, O Lord" and many more.

Though her hymn writing declined in later years, Fanny was active in speaking engagements and missionary work among America's urban poor almost until the day of her death in 1915. She sought to bring others to her Savior not only through her hymns but through her personal life as well.

Fanny wrote enough hymns over the course of her lifetime to fill fifteen complete hymnals. Of course, many of those have been forgotten today, but a large number of them remain favorites of Christians all over the world.

*Recommended reading: John Woodbridge, general editor,* More Than Conquerors: Portraits of Believers from All Walks of Life *(Chicago: Moody, 1992).*

# TOO WEAK *to* GO

*I*n February of 1914, Amy Carmichael wrote to friends
that she did not expect to be among them within a week.
*She expected to instead be inside an Indian prison on a charge
of kidnapping.*

*And, indeed, she was a kidnapper. Thirteen years earlier, in 1901, Amy had sheltered her
first temple runaway in India. Temple children were dedicated to the gods and forced to satisfy the lusts of depraved men to earn money for the priests. Over the years, Amy had rescued
many children, often at the cost of personal exhaustion and danger.*

*One of her latest rescues was that of five-year-old Kohila. Kohila's guardians were now
agitating to have the child back. Amy refused to return the child to certain abuse and instead
made plans to cause the girl to "disappear" to a safe
place.*

*Amy was too well-known to spirit Kohila away her-
self, so she arranged for someone else to do it. The plot
was discovered, and charges were brought against Amy.
She was facing a seven-year prison term.*

## Amy Carmichael

**Born:** December 16, 1867,
in Millisle, Northern Ireland

**Education:** Attended Har-
rogate and other schools

**Married:** Did not marry

**Children:** None

**Died:** January 18, 1951,
in Dohnavur, India

**Quote:** "Nothing too precious for Jesus."

## An Unlikely Heroine

Amy Carmichael was an unlikely heroine. She
suffered from neuralgia, a disease of the nerves
that made her whole body weak and achy and often put her in bed for weeks on end. Her friends
thought she was foolish when she announced in
1892 that she was going to be a missionary. They
predicted that she would soon be back in England
permanently. But Amy was sure that God had
called her to go overseas.

135

Courtesy Christian History Institute archives

*Hindus denied that children were forced to prostitute at temples like this one, but Amy had evidence and rescued children from these environs.*

All of her life, she had been learning to listen to His voice. One of the first incidents occurred when she was a child growing up in Ireland. Her mother had said that if Amy prayed, the Lord would answer. Amy had brown eyes, and that night she prayed for them to be blue. In the morning she jumped out of bed and ran to the mirror. Mrs. Carmichael heard her wail in disappointment.

It took several minutes of careful explanation before Amy understood that "no" was an answer too. God meant for Amy to have brown eyes for a reason. Just what the reason was, she might never know, but in the meantime, said Mrs. Carmichael, brown eyes were perfectly lovely. Amy wasn't so sure. Smiling Irish blue would always be her preference, even if God said "no."

## Amy's Youthful Escapades

There was a bit of rebel in Amy. If trouble developed at the Carmichael house, she was almost sure to be a ringleader in it. One time, animal squeaks interrupted family devotions. Amy feigned ignorance, but the truth eventually came out. She had been keeping a frozen mouse in her pocket, and it had revived. Another time she led her brothers and sisters in a challenge to see how many poisonous laburnum pods they could eat before they died. Fortunately, they emerged with little more than upset stomachs.

When the Carmichaels hired a governess, the children sensed that she did not like them, and Amy led her siblings in making life unbearable for the young woman. They put bugs in her tea and toads in her bed. Finally, the governess quit. Unrepentant, Amy watched as tears coursed down her mother's cheeks, but eventually hardness melted, and she ran to her mother, flung her arms around her and sobbed for forgiveness.

The most dangerous of all of Amy's escapades was the time when she and her brothers were rowing their boat on Stranford Lough and passed beyond the boundaries that had been set for them and into a deadly current. The water swept their boat toward a sandbar, and though the boys strained manfully, the current dragged them irresistibly on. "Sing!" shouted Ernest. Amy raised her voice wildly in the first words that came to mind—"He leadeth me, O blessed thought"—and the boys, straining futilely at the oars, joined her. Fortunately, the song was heard by a coastguard crew and a rescue party saved them.

When Amy was thirteen, she was sent to boarding school. One night, the Great Comet of 1882 was supposed to put in a spectacular appearance in the night sky, and Amy asked but was refused permission for her and the other girls to sit up and watch the comet pass over. Amy led the others in a daring plan. They would wait until the teachers were asleep and then sneak to the attic window for a look. One by one the other girls dropped off to sleep, but Amy kept herself awake. When she thought enough time had passed, she roused the others and led them up the attic stairs. She flung open the door, only to find all of the teachers there, observing the comet themselves.

## Amy's World Caves In

While she was in school, Amy thought that she already loved Christ, but around 1883 an evangelist showed her that she needed a Savior, and she gave her heart to Christ. After three years of boarding school, she returned home because her parents no longer had the money to support her education. Mrs. Carmichael took the sixteen-year-old girl out to buy a dress, and Amy found a beautiful one—royal blue—but she turned away from it. Her mother was surprised, but Amy explained that clothes were no longer as important to her as they had once been now that Christ had given her new purpose in life. She was willing to wait a year until her parents were better able to afford new clothes for her. Amy never got that dress, however, because a year later Mr. Carmichael died unexpectedly.

That year, 1885, Amy started classes and prayer groups for Belfast ragamuffins. She also began a Sunday ministry to the "shawlies," factory girls who were so poor that they could not afford hats to wear to church and wore shawls instead. Respectable people didn't want anything to do with them, but Amy saw that they needed Christ just the same as their "betters." Eventually so many shawlies attended Amy's classes that she had to find a building large enough to hold 300 and more.

The Carmichaels lost all of their money through financial reverses, and a change became necessary. In 1888 Mrs. Carmichael decided to move to England to work for Mr. Jacob McGill, whom they called "Uncle Jacob." Amy and another sister joined her. Uncle Jacob asked Amy to teach his mill workers about Christ, and she threw herself into the work, living near the mill in an apartment that was infested with cockroaches and bed bugs.

Unfortunately, Amy was constantly sick with neuralgia and had to lie in bed for days at a time. It was clear that she had to give up the work. Mr. Wilson, the founder of Keswick, a movement to help men become holy, invited Amy to stay with him and his grown children

*Mary, Maud, and I had some time together before Mr. Arden left and one day toward the end of the first week one of them said, "You have been here for a week and you haven't said one word about the Lord Jesus Christ." I shall never forget the reproach in her voice, or how deeply I felt the rebuke. It was true that I had not said one word. The girls were like butterflies, pretty and dressy, and I had been shy of them both. I had no idea they cared for the things of Christ, and had thought I should wait till I knew them better before speaking of these things. But they told me now that they had been converted a little while ago and were hungry.*

(cont'd on next page)

at Broughton Grange, Cumberland, and he became like a second father to her. Amy would become the first missionary sponsored by Keswick.

## Commanded to Go

For years Amy wanted to be a missionary in a heathen country. The desire grew so strong that it hurt. She prayed about it and wrote down the reasons she thought it wasn't God's intention for her. One of the first things on the list was her sickness.

She spoke to Mr. Wilson about it, and after praying with him, Amy went back to her room and heard the Lord speak as if He were standing in her room, saying, "Go ye."

"Surely, Lord, You don't mean it," she said.

Again the voice said, "Go ye."

Amy agreed. But where? And would her mother approve? She wrote to her mother, and Mrs. Carmichael replied that the Lord had already spoken to her about it and told her that she must let Amy go.

For over a year Amy tried to find a place to go, but no one wanted her. Finally, Mr. Wilson suggested Japan. He wrote to the Buxtons, missionaries in Japan, to see if they could use Amy. Amy felt convinced that she ought to leave right away, although she had received no reply. She left with three other missionary ladies on March 3, 1893. Tears scalded her face as she sailed away; it was hard to say good-bye to those she loved.

The trip was not without its chances to witness for Christ. Amy faced the dirt and insects of one ship so cheerfully that the captain was converted as a result. When she finally reached Shanghai, the reply from the Buxtons was waiting for her. Yes, they wanted her. So Amy crossed over to Japan.

Through a mixup of dates, no one met her at the station. It began to rain, and Amy laughed at her plight. After an hour of trying to make the Japanese understand her, she prayed that the Lord would send someone to help. Minutes later, an American came by and sent her on her way. It was a miracle that the man had appeared when he did, since at the time there were only 3,000 Westerners in all of Japan.

*The friend who had led them to Christ had said I would be coming by the next boat and that I would help them. So all the time that I had been thinking of them as pretty butterflies, they were really hungry lambs. I have never forgotten the shame of that hour. But we have a forgiving Lord. He gave us a wonderful time together.*

*—Amy Carmichael*

## Spirit of a Fox

Even before she learned the Japanese language, Amy went out to witness. Her interpreter, Misaki San, suggested that Amy wear a kimono, but Amy was cold and her neuralgia was bothering her. She preferred her Western dress and kept it on. The two girls visited a sick old woman who seemed interested in the gospel. Just as Amy was about to ask the woman if she wanted to repent, the woman caught sight of Amy's fur-lined gloves and asked what they were, distracted from the gospel message. Driving home, Amy wept bitter tears. Never again would she risk so much for so little, she promised. From then on she wore Japanese clothing while witnessing.

On another occasion, Amy and Misaki San were asked to send the spirit of a fox out of a violent and murderous man. Village priests had tried their formulas and tortures without success. Trusting that the Lord could drive demons away, the two girls prayed and went boldly into the man's room. As soon as they mentioned the name of Jesus, the man went into an uncontrollable rage. If he had not been tied down, he would have leapt at them. The two girls were thrust from the room. They were perplexed, but they soon recovered their confidence. They assured the man's wife that they would pray until the spirit left and asked her to send a message when it was gone. Within an hour, they had received word that the demon had departed. The next day, the man himself summoned them, and over the next few days they explained the way of Christ to him and he became a Christian.

## Saving Souls by Numbers

Once when Amy was about to visit the Buddhist village of Hirose, she asked the Lord what she should ask of Him before she went. She felt impressed to pray for the salvation of one soul. While they were in Hirose, a young silk-weaver heard their message and became a Christian.

Amy's neuralgia kept her in bed for a month after that, but the next time she went out, she again felt that she must pray, and the Lord told her to ask for two souls. The silk-weaver brought two friends to meet with them in Hirose, and they gave themselves to Jesus.

Two weeks later, Amy felt impressed to ask for four souls. This was more souls than many missionaries saw won to Christ in a year. The visit to Hirose went badly, and Amy wondered if she had mistaken an arithmetical progression for the leading of the Lord. No one in the village seemed interested in the gospel.

Misaki San reminded Amy that the evening service still lay ahead, but not many came to the service. Those few who did seemed distracted. Amy was almost in tears. She wanted to run out and bury herself in the snow.

Suddenly, the spirit of the service changed. A woman spoke up and asked the way to Christ, and then her son came in and committed himself to the new religion also. At the home of some Christians that evening, another woman accepted Christ, and the next morning a fourth was converted. God had answered Amy's prayer, even at the last minute.

Again Amy was ill after her trip to Hirose, this time for a month and a half. For two weeks the Lord impressed on her that she should ask for eight souls. The other missionaries chided her. "It is not faith," they said, "but presumption." With astonishment, Amy heard them advise her just to pray for a blessing. "Then you won't be disappointed," they said.

Amy insisted that the Lord Himself had wrestled with her. She was terrified, she said, and would never ask this in her own strength. An older missionary agreed with her. He read God's promise from Jeremiah that says that nothing is too hard for the Lord. "Let us pray for her," he said. Needless to say, eight souls were converted to belief in Christ on the next visit.

Amy did not receive any more impressions to pray for the salvation of specific numbers of souls after that. In fact, her neuralgia became so bad that a doctor told her she must leave Japan for a more suitable climate. She sailed from Japan in July 1894.

## On to Sunny India

Again Amy was unsure where she should go. She visited Ceylon, where sunny days helped her recover. Then, learning that Mr. Wilson was ill, she returned to England. He suggested that she work in sunny India, where her health would suffer less.

Immediately she rejected the idea. It was too easy and therefore must not be God's will. Mr. Wilson retorted that it might very well be God's will to use her someplace where she could remain healthy enough to get something done for Him. Immediately Amy realized that she was making the decision without prayer because she had hoped to return to Japan. Her doctors had closed the door to the land of the rising sun once and for all. But India, yes—she might go there. And so Amy sailed to warm Bangalore in October of 1895.

It was in India that Amy learned about the temple children. Even Christians opposed Amy when she stepped into the struggle to end the wicked service required of the little girls. They thought she exaggerated the situation.

Indeed, the truth of what went on behind the scenes was so hard to get at that Amy found that she had to pretend to be an Indian and visit the temples herself. Dressed in a sari with her skin stained, she could pass as a Hindu. It was then that she understood why God had given her brown eyes: Blue eyes would have been a dead giveaway!

Amy's experiences were proof that the Lord truly was in charge of her life. Even when she became permanently bedridden toward the end of her life, God had plans for her. She wrote books that became a deep spiritual witness to others.

She did not serve the seven-year prison term for Kohila's kidnapping. Instead, a telegram arrived on February 7, 1914, stating simply, "Criminal case dismissed." No explanation was ever given for the change, but those who know Amy's Lord suspected that He had a hand in the decision.

Amy lived to be eighty-three. She died on January 18, 1951, in Dohnavur, India, much beloved. She wrote poetry almost to the end of her life and encouraged those around her with her cheerful words.

*Recommended reading: Rebecca Henry Davis,* With Daring Faith: A Biography of Amy Carmichael *(Greenville, SC: Bob Jones University, 1987).*

# VICTORY *on* *the* MOUNTAINS *of* DEATH

*E*vie Brand burst into tears. She pleaded with the mission board, but its members would not yield. Rules were rules, they said. She was too old to go back to India. She must retire.

The decision was hard for the board too. Evie had long sacrificed comforts and family for the sake of her mission work. With her husband, Jesse, she had pioneered in the Mountains of Death until he died of fever. Year after year, she had lived entirely on a small inheritance and set aside her official salary to buy land for the mission. But ever since Jesse had died, the mission had not been sure what to do with her. The one task she wanted—to open new work in the Mountains of Death—was denied her because she was elderly, single . . . and opinionated.

## Evie Brand

**Born:** 1879 in England
**Education:** Attended English schools
**Married:** Jesse Brand in 1913
**Children:** Two
**Died:** December 18, 1974, in Karigiri, India
**Quote:** "Let me be like that, Lord, flowering best when life seems most dry and dead."

From the board's point of view, it was senseless to appoint a sixty-eight-year-old woman to another five-year term, but years ago, Jesse and Evie had vowed to reach five mountain ranges with the gospel. Four still had to be reached. Evie felt that God was calling her to fulfill that vow.

Evie grasped at one last straw. "Please just send me back for one year," she pleaded. "I promise not to make any more trouble. At the end of one year I will retire." Reluctantly, the board agreed. Had they known the secret plan that Evie had confided to her daughter, they almost surely would have refused.

## Life Begins at Seventy

Evie said good-bye to her friends and relatives in England and was back in India by January of 1947. The mission appointed her to a station in

Courtesy Dorothy Clarke Wilson,
*Granny Brand* (Chappaqua, NY, 1976).
Used by permission of Paul Brand.

*Evie on horseback*

the plains. This time Evie did not mind the plains as much as she had in previous times, because it was only for a year.

Camping in the Kalryan range on every holiday, Evie plotted her next move. Her son designed a little house for her, and she scrounged building materials and organized it into loads light enough for helpers to carry up the mountains.

When Evie's year with the mission drew to a close, her fellow missionaries gathered to wish her a tearful good-bye and presented her with a parting gift: a lovely lamp. Then came the shock. Evie gleefully informed everyone that she was retiring from the mission—retiring to take up independent work in the mountains, to fulfill the commission that she and Jesse had undertaken years before. Her colleagues' protests and warnings fell on deaf ears. As far as Evie was concerned, life begins at seventy.

## Frilly Dresses

Strictly speaking, life begins a little sooner. Evelyn Harris was born in England in 1879. Her father was a well-to-do merchant. As a young woman, Evie cut a fine figure in plumed hats and frilly dresses. The Harrises were involved in missions, street work and charities. Mr. Harris protected his daughters—all ten of them—even trying to dissuade them from marriages that would take them away from him, but one by one they left the nest and started families of their own.

Evie, one of the youngest, loved to paint. Her idol was the painter John Joseph Turner, who seemed able to capture light itself on his canvases. To the end of her days, she sketched and painted with gusto. But when she entered her twenties, she found that art did not feed her soul.

Evie was thirty when she spent a few weeks in Australia with her sister Flossie. Sailing home, she sensed a divine calling to be a missionary. But how was she to break the news to her father?

The arrival of a young missionary from India in 1906 helped. Evie found Jesse Brand to be too intense for her taste. But at a missionary meeting, he seemed to look directly at her as he described the filth and squalor on the mission field. She heard an unspoken question in his words: Could she, a fashionable girl, handle such things? Defiance rose within her. Yes, with God's help she could! And she was just riled up enough to tell her father so.

Mr. Harris took Evie's announcement hard. She wanted to be a missionary? Weren't there enough lost souls in London? Evie insisted that she had to obey God's call. Finally, Mr. Harris yielded, but he insisted that she must allow him to provide her entire support.

At her farewell party, Evie wore her usual finery. "She looks more like an actress than a missionary," commented an amused bystander.

## Wedding Bells in Madras

Evie was assigned to Madras in the plains of India, and she soon discovered that Jesse Brand had been transferred there also. Daily contact with him changed her opinion of him. She fell in love with him and with his vision for the Mountains of Death.

Then she overheard a private conversation and learned that Jesse was engaged. Hot and shaking, she fled to her bathroom, where she poured cool water over herself. She had made a fool of herself! Her heart grew dry. Looking at the flowers blooming brilliantly in India's dry season, she prayed, "Let me be like that, Lord, flowering best when life seems most dry and dead."

Language study took Evie to the hills, and while she was there, Jesse wrote to her to tell her that his engagement had been called off. He asked Evie to marry him. They would work in the Mountains of Death together.

Evie's honeymoon in 1913 was a "perfect" introduction to life in the hills. Dressed in wedding white, she followed Jesse to the canvas *dholi* (carrier) that was to carry her into the hills. The bearers had gone off to hunt a wild pig. New bearers were found, but thunder rumbled in the sky. The heat wilted Evie's dress, and she tried not to give way to terror as the *dholi* bearers lurched along steep precipices. Great drops of rain splashed upon her, and thorns tore her dress. Rain turned her *dholi* into a bathtub. When she dismounted to walk, she sank deep into mud holes. They lost their way in the dark and shouted until someone brought a lamp. They were glad when they finally reached the shelter of a hut.

## Mountains of Death

That was the beginning of their work in the mountains. It was not glamorous work. At the start, only one young man who was dying gave his heart to Christ. It would be seven years before they saw another convert on the Kolli range. Because Hindu priests

*Paul and Margaret brought their children and a fine turkey to the hills for Christmas with Granny. "We'll have the turkey for the evening meal," Evie decided. . . .*

*Suddenly, men burst into the living room bearing a stretcher. On it lay a sick woman, her eyes staring, her lips cracked and open. Granny felt for a pulse. "Typhoid," she said. "Water! No—bring me buttermilk. It's more nourishing." . . .*

*"Mother," said Paul, thinking of the waiting children and the shriveling turkey, "don't you think perhaps since it is Christmas we could have some turkey with the children and let someone else give this woman her fluid?"*

*(cont'd on next page)*

feared to lose their influence over the people and also their revenue, they opposed the gospel. People hungered to follow the Swami Yesu (Jesus), because Jesse was able to heal them of many diseases, but the priests frightened them away from the new religion.

Jesse energetically taught the people better methods of farming, treated their sick, built houses, imported seeds for new and better crops and fought tax battles for them. He showed Evie the five ranges of mountains that he hoped to win for Christ: their own Kolli, of course, and beyond it Pachais, Kalryan, Peria Malai and Chitteris.

Jesse and Evie went from village to village preaching the gospel and tending to the sick, but the people always pulled back from Christianity out of fear of the Hindu priests. A breakthrough finally came when a priest developed a fever. Jesse hurried to his aid. As the man died, he entrusted his children to the Brands. The Jesus God must be the true one, he said, because the Brands alone had come to help him in his hour of death.

The people marveled at a God who made Jesse take in an enemy's orphaned children rather than abandon them to die. Evie eventually became mother to many abandoned Indian children, although rumors said that she took them to eat them. Through her motherly love, a small Christian community was born.

Still, the progress of the gospel in the hills remained painfully slow. Painful too was the need for Jesse and Evie to leave their two children, Paul and Connie, in England for schooling in 1923. Evie said that something "just died in me" the day she had to say good-bye to them. It was the hardest test of loyalty God had ever given her.

## Widowed by Blackwater Fever

Not many years passed before Paul and Connie received word that their father was dead. Jesse had contracted blackwater fever. Although Evie felt hollow inside, she prayed that the Lord would allow Jesse's death to win more souls than his life had. Hindu and Christian alike mourned the man who had poured out love on them, and they vied with each other for the usually contemptible job of digging his grave and lowering his dead body into it.

Evie struggled alone with the mission work until a replacement for Jesse was found. Although she had lost Jesse, she sometimes found him to be very near. He had once promised to show her a shortcut to a certain village. "Now he'll not be able to," she lamented. She was wrong. As she was riding Jesse's horse one day, it remembered the path and carried her along it.

After a visit with her children in England, Evie determined to return to the Kollis Mountains. The mission leaders were uneasy. Would it work? They were right to ask, but Evie had expected her coworkers to approach the work just as Jesse would have. When they didn't, she spoke up and tension resulted. She pleaded with the mission leaders to be allowed to start a new work on one of the other ranges. They refused. Mountain work did not show good returns, they said. They transferred her to the plains instead. At times she considered leaving the mission to strike out on her own, but circumstances always held her back—that is, until she retired.

*Evie turned on him with a look of absolute fury. "How dare you, Paul! How can you talk about turkey when there's a woman down here dying!" . . .*

*In the morning the woman was much better. Evie, with an instinct for the simple, right remedy, had saved her life without expensive medicines that could not have been procured in time anyhow.*

*The next day, one of her grandchildren asked, "Mummy, have we had Christmas?"*

## Fulfilling Jesse's Dream

Rejoicing in her "retirement," Evie began to fulfill Jesse's dream. Everyone called her "Granny," but she felt young. Just as in the old times, she traveled from village to village, riding a hill pony, camping, teaching, dispensing medicine and rescuing abandoned children.

The work was harder now, and her body was more frail. One time she was dropped by her carriers and hit her head on a rock. She never completely recovered her balance after that, and she took to walking with bamboo canes. Yet she was full of joy and laughter. "Praise God!" she exclaimed continually.

Despite broken bones, fevers and infirmities, Evie labored on. In fifteen years, she almost eradicated the parasitic Guinea worm from the Kalryan range. Through her efforts, the five ranges were evangelized and mission work was planted on each. Evie lengthened her sights, adding two more ranges. She insisted that this extraordinary accomplishment was God's doing, not hers.

Courtesy Dorothy Clarke Wilson, *Granny Brand* (Chappaqua, NY, 1976). Used by permission of Paul Brand.

*In her old age, Evie walked with canes.*

Wherever she was, Evie proclaimed Christ. When in the hospital with a broken hip at age seventy-five, she wheeled herself from room to room (or scooted on a carpet!) and talked to the other patients. She painted landscapes for them, and her pictures soon found their way onto hospital walls. Her bones knit back together in record time, and back she went to the mountains to fight the marijuana growers and seek out substitute cash crops for them.

When Evie was about ninety years old, her son Paul, who later went on to become a noted physician and author, visited her in the mountains and found her looking not older but younger. It was her smile, brighter than ever, that made the difference. "This is how to grow old," he wrote. "Allow everything else to fall away, until those around you see just love."

In 1974 Evie tore some ligaments in her knee and had to go to the plains for treatment. Before she could return to her beloved mountains, her speech became jumbled and her memory failed. Seven days later, on December 18, 1974, she died.

The next day her body was taken back to the hills and laid beside Jesse's as a multitude wept. The woman who had been declared too old to stay in India had carried on for twenty-four years more, working almost to the day of her death.

*Recommended reading: Dorothy Clarke Wilson,* Granny Brand: Her Story *(New York: Christian Herald Books, 1976).*

# Part 7
## First and Foremost

*They blazed
trails for others
to follow.*

# FIRST
# BIBLICAL
# ARCHAEOLOGIST

*A*t Christmastime, "Manger Square" in Bethlehem is thronged with pilgrims coming to worship at the Church of the Nativity. At Easter, Christians follow the Via Dolorosa to the Church of the Holy Sepulcher in Jerusalem. Both of these ancient churches in the Holy Land are intimately connected with the Empress Helena, mother of the first Christian emperor, Constantine.

## Helena

**Born:** Third century, probably in Asia Minor

**Education:** Unknown

**Married:** Constantius Chlorus, date unknown

**Children:** One

**Died:** Around 330

**Quote:** "She became under his [Constantine's] influence such a devout servant of God that one might believe her to have been from her very childhood a disciple of the Redeemer of mankind."

Much of Helena's story is obscure or unknown, including the date and place of her birth. Some theorize that since Constantine later named a town in Asia Minor Helenopolis in her honor, she was born there and was the daughter of an innkeeper. However, the British have an ancient tradition that says that Helena was the daughter of King Coel of Colchester (later immortalized in Mother Goose's "Old King Cole, the Merry Old Soul"). It is known that there was a Christian church in Colchester in AD 250, about the time when Helena was born, and it is possible that she became a Christian as a young woman.

## Marriage and Divorce

It is also unclear when Helena met the Roman soldier Constantius Chlorus or if the two were ever officially married. What is certain is that Constantius and Helena were Constantine's parents. When Constantius became caesar of Gaul, Spain and Britain in 292, he divorced Helena in

*T*here are advantages to having a son who is the ruler of the world and can order people into action. Because of her relationship to Constantine, Helena could count on assistance when she traveled to Jerusalem and began hunting for the places where Jesus Christ lived and died. Although she was no professional and may have misidentified sites, Helena was the first biblical archaeologist on record.

order to marry Theodora, daughter of his patron, Maximian. It was an obvious and coldly calculated political move designed to promote Constantius' career.

Helena's son Constantine spent a lot of his time at the court of the emperor Diocletian and became a soldier like his father. When his troops later proclaimed Constantine emperor in 306, one of his first acts was to call his mother from political exile (she was apparently removed from center stage after her divorce from Constantius) and give her honors befitting the mother of the Roman emperor. When Constantine embraced Christianity, Helena gave her strong support and encouragement.

It was not all peace and prosperity in the imperial court, however. For reasons that are shrouded in darkness and uncertainty, in 326 Constantine had his oldest son Crispus and his wife Fausta executed. He later was apparently plagued with guilt; it is possible that Helena was responsible for convincing him of his sin. This sense of guilt and a need for repentance might have been what caused Constantine to send Helena on her mission to the Holy Land.

## An Eighty-Year-Old's Holy Mission

When she was almost eighty years old, Helena traveled throughout Palestine and the eastern imperial provinces, encouraging the establishment and spread of the Christian faith. In Palestine she sought out the original sites that were associated with the life of Jesus, and she oversaw the construction of churches that Constantine had ordered to be built at such sites as Bethlehem, Calvary, Olivet and Bethany. A pagan temple to Aphrodite that had been built on the site of Jesus' resurrection was torn down and replaced by the Church of the Holy Sepulcher. Later legends arose that in the tomb beneath the the church, Helena had also discovered the actual cross on which Christ had died.

Helena's tour of the Holy Land was important because it became a pattern for Christian pilgrims throughout the Middle Ages and into our own day as she sought to discover and honor the places where Jesus had lived. In light of her investigations, she has been called the first biblical archaeologist. The churches she built were a focus for pilgrims for centuries.

Courtesy John B. Firth, *Constantine the Great* (New York: Putnam, 1905)

*Constantine, son of Helena*

*Recommended reading: Jan Willem Drijvers,* Helena Augusta: The Mother of Constantine the Great and the Legend of Her Finding of the True Cross *(Leiden, NY: E.J. Brill, 1992).*

# *The* WALK THAT PAVED *the* WAY

*I*t was dark when teenaged Mary and her mother walked home from the church meeting. As they carefully kept to the path in the darkness, Mary recalled the preacher's words from Psalm 119:105, "[God's W]ord is a lamp unto my feet, and a light unto my path." How Mary wished that she had a Bible of her own so that she could learn more of God's Word!

## Mary Jones

**Born:** December 16, 1784, in Llanfihangel-y-Pennant, Wales

**Education:** Attended a village school for a few years

**Married:** Unknown

**Children:** Unknown

**Died:** Around 1866

**Quote:** "Surely a society might be formed for the purpose [of getting Bibles to the needy]! But if for Wales, why not for Great Britain? Why not for the world?" (Rev. Joseph Hughes)

## Focused on the Word

Mary Jones was born on December 16, 1784, in the Welsh village of Llanfihangel-y-Pennant, at the foot of Wales' famous Cedar Idris. Her father was a weaver who died when Mary was four. Mary and her mother were poor, but they got on the best that they could.

When Mary was about eight years old, a school was established about an hour's walk from Llanfihangel. Mary took the two-hour round-trip walk each day and progressed well in reading. She wished she had a Bible to read, but her mother told her it was too expensive.

One of their neighbors did have a Bible, though, and every Saturday afternoon Mary went to read Mrs. Evans' Bible for several hours. Mrs. Evans was not poor like the Joneses; she lived in a house that was filled with beautiful things. Mary, however, was

Courtesy W.J. Loftie, *London City*
(London: Leadenhall Press, 1891)

*The British and Foreign Bible Society building in London in the late 1800s*

not distracted by the comfort and riches around her. She read through book after book of the Bible.

## First Chickens and Eggs

One day as Mary was washing her family's clothes in the river, she got the idea that she could earn some money by washing for other people as well. Then she could save enough money for a Bible of her own.

When Mrs. Evans heard of Mary's plan, she gave Mary some chickens to raise. When the chicks became hens, Mary could earn money by selling the eggs. Mary soon found other ways for earning money too—looking after children, weeding gardens and knitting socks.

After six years of careful saving, Mary finally had enough money to buy a Bible, but there were none to be bought in her village. Rev. Thomas Charles sold them in Bala, but that was over twenty-five miles away!

In the summer of 1800, when she was not yet sixteen years old, Mary set out alone with the money she had earned and made the long walk to Bala. She even took off her shoes and carried them so that they wouldn't wear out. Although it was a long and difficult walk, Mary was so full of anticipation that she barely noticed.

## Too Late, Mary

When she finally arrived and found Rev. Charles, he told her that he only had one Bible left and it had already been promised to someone else. Mary could not hold back her tears. After working and saving for six years and then walking for over twenty-five miles, she could not help but be extremely disappointed. All her work seemed wasted!

But when Rev. Charles heard that Mary had worked for six years to save enough money to buy a Bible, he made her take his last one. The other person could wait a little longer.

## Mary Sparks a Vision

Rev. Charles was tremendously moved by Mary's efforts to obtain a Bible. Many people in Wales and throughout Britain were coming to Christ, and Bibles needed to be more readily available for these new converts. In December of 1802, Rev. Charles was in London and laid before a committee of the Religious Tract Society the desperate need for Bibles in the Welsh language. Rev. Charles told the committee about Mary Jones and all that she had done in order to get a Bible of her own.

Though the committee appreciated the need for Bible distribution, neither the Religious Tract Society nor the Society for the Promotion of Christian Knowledge felt like they could meet the demand. Rev. Joseph Hughes suggested that "a society might be formed for the purpose—and if for Wales, why not for the Kingdom; why not for the whole world?"

Fifteen months later, on March 7, 1804, The British and Foreign Bible Society (BFBS) was formed "for the wider distribution of the Scriptures, without note or comment." The Clapham Sect, a group of influential evangelicals including William Wilberforce, were important in establishing the BFBS. The Society determined to distribute Bibles throughout the whole world, and within a few months the Gospel of John was issued in the Mohawk language.

The Society was not interested in fostering any particular interpretation of the Bible; it was solely concerned that people have access to the Scriptures. The governing committee was interdenominational and included fifteen Anglicans, fifteen Free Church laymen and six representatives of foreign churches.

*It is one of the curiosities of human psychology that we often want most what we can't get. When Bibles were scarce, people suffered a great deal to obtain one. Mary Jones is an example of such a longing. Now that Bibles are readily available in dozens of versions, even those who have them all too often don't open them.*

## To All the World

Auxiliary local groups arose throughout Britain to raise funds and distribute Bibles in their localities. Similar Bible societies were formed in Germany, the Netherlands, Denmark, Russia, France, Greece and the United States. The Bible societies worked closely with growing missionary endeavors to translate the Bible into other languages. All of the great missionaries, including William Carey in India, Robert Morris in China, Henry Martyn in India and Adoniram Judson in Burma, relied on the Bible societies for support.

By 1907 the BFBS had distributed 203,931,768 Bibles, Testaments and portions of Scripture throughout the world. This worldwide movement of Bible translation that had grown out of the local needs of people such as young Mary Jones affected men and women of many nationalities and church traditions.

Mary died at the age of eighty-two. In the town of Llanfihangel, a monument has been erected with the following inscription in English and Welsh: "To the remembrance of Mary Jones, who in 1800 at the age of 16, walked from here to Bala, in order to buy a Bible from Rev. Charles in the Welsh language. This event was the cause of the foundation of The British and Foreign Bible Society. The Bible Mary bought from Rev. Charles is now in the Cambridge University Library."

*Recommended reading: Mig Holder,* Mary Jones and Her Bible *(Swindon, UK: Bible Society [The British and Foreign Bible Society], 1992).*

# SHE WILLINGLY WENT to PRISON

"*You are born to be a light to the blind, speech to the dumb and feet to the lame.*"

*In 1798 eighteen-year-old Elizabeth Gurney heard this prediction with wonder. Had not her friend Deborah Darby gone too far? Members of the Society of Friends, commonly called "Quakers," accepted that the Holy Spirit spoke to them through one another, but Deborah's words seemed overly bold for a time in which women were not allowed much scope of action.*

*Earlier that same year Elizabeth had fallen under conviction in a meeting led by a Quaker from the United States. So deep was the impression left on her that she had wept in the carriage most of the way home, where she confided to her diary, "Today I have felt that there is a God." Yet no compelling sense of purpose came to her.*

*Nor did it when Deborah spoke to her. Nonetheless, Elizabeth made herself useful where she could, starting a Sunday school with just one boy in attendance. The class quickly grew to eighty. She also provided the poor with food and clothes and read to them from the Scriptures.*

## Elizabeth Fry

**Born:** May 21, 1780, in Norwich, England
**Education:** Attended Quaker schools
**Married:** Joseph Fry on August 19, 1800
**Children:** Ten
**Died:** October 12, 1845, in Kent, England
**Quote:** "Charity to the Soul is the Soul of Charity."

## Be Careful, Elizabeth

Born in 1780, Elizabeth had had to make herself useful at an early age. Her mother died when Elizabeth was just twelve, and much of the responsibility of raising her younger siblings fell on Elizabeth.

When banker Joseph Fry proposed marriage in 1799, Elizabeth hesitated, hoping for illumina-

*"Nothing short of the Holy Spirit can really help forward the cause of righteousness on earth," said Elizabeth Fry. She believed herself to be an agent of that cause, and indeed she was. On the evenings before their transportation to the colonies, women commonly rioted in Newgate prison, but Elizabeth overcame the practice by visiting them and reading to them from the Bible on those days.*

tion from the Lord. Since she received no specific guidance, she accepted the offer and over the course of their marriage bore ten children.

It was not until after the tenth child was born that Elizabeth caught a glimpse of her mission. In 1817 her brother-in-law, Thomas Fowell Buxton, a member of Parliament, suggested that she visit the women's section of Newgate prison. Crime was on the rise, and English prisons were overcrowded. Perhaps some remedy was possible.

Her friends cautioned Elizabeth not to go. The female prisoners were so violent that they would snatch clothes off of visitors' backs, heckle them and steal their valuables. The governor of Newgate himself didn't dare to approach them. But Elizabeth was determined to take action. This was just the challenge she craved. Having visited a prison before, she wasn't to be frightened off. Had not the Lord commanded His people to remember those who were in prison? So Elizabeth entered Newgate, refusing to even take off her watch, which, incidentally, was not stolen.

Nothing had prepared Elizabeth for what she found inside the prison. Hundreds of drunken, rag-clad women crowded into four rooms that were built to hold half their number. Innocent girls awaited trial side by side with hardened prostitutes and thieves. Children, whose only fault was having nowhere else to go, might have envied barnyard animals their stables, and naked babies who had been born in prison fussed and squalled.

The turnkeys (or guards), who made their income "shaking down" prisoners, sold a few amenities—even booze—to the prisoners. Bathing supplies were scarce, and lice swarmed in the women's clothes and hair. The daily ration of food was one small loaf of bread per person. There was no medicine, and sick women were dumped on dirty straw without so much as a bed to rest upon. Death by "prison fever" (typhus) was common.

Discipline was nonexistent within the prison. Bullies ran the wards, and fights and curses erupted regularly. Many of the women strutted around in men's clothes, and even the tough male prisoners, who mingled with the women during the day, were appalled by their behavior.

## An Appeal Through the Babies

Elizabeth made her appeal to the female prisoners through the babies. Surely the women desired better than this squalor for their little ones! And indeed they did—but they had no income, no education, no discipline and no hope. Elizabeth promised to help them, and they listened respectfully, recognizing her plain dress as a religious uniform. She could project so much pathos into her voice that hardened criminals melted and cool observers found themselves in tears.

Courtesy Christian History Institute archives

*Elizabeth reads to prisoners.*

Drawing on her own resources and the funds of others, Elizabeth gathered supplies and formed committees. She organized classes in knitting and sewing. Soon the women were able to sell their piecework and earn a little money for soap and food.

After fierce haggling she obtained a room for a school. The best educated among them was designated to teach, and each day Elizabeth read aloud to them from the Bible, hoping that the salvation story would sink into their minds and convert them. A few sought Christ's pardon and found new peace.

## Teaching Self-Discipline

The Quakeress convinced the prison authorities to appoint matrons in place of male turnkeys. With steely determination, she enforced rules that the prisoners themselves voted on. She had them elect leaders to keep order among themselves, and soon Newgate's female wards evidenced unprecedented decorum. The transformation was so extraordinary that world leaders heard of it and consulted with Elizabeth.

At that time, many convicts were transported from England to Australia. The system was especially brutal to women, for the ships were not outfitted to accommodate them. Destitute when they reached Australia, some women resorted to prostitution as a means to fill their stomachs. Elizabeth agitated for reforms. Meanwhile, for twenty years she and her committee visited every transportation ship before it sailed, ensuring that the women had cloth and thread so that on the long voyage they might make things that they could then sell in the colony when they arrived. Thanks in part to her, the transportation of prisoners was exposed as an inhumane institution, and shortly after her death it was outlawed.

Elizabeth's reforms prompted other advances as well. Theodore Fliedner, a young German pastor, imported her ideas to Germany. To succor ill women, he trained nurses. Elizabeth, impressed by the idea, in 1840 founded the Institute of Nursing Sisters to work among the poor. The nurses were given rudimentary training at Guy's Hospital in London.

Fittingly, one of these sisters nursed Elizabeth in her last illness. She died at age sixty-five. Her actions, spurred by faith, had fulfilled Deborah Darby's vision: She had become a voice for prisoners who could not speak for themselves.

*Recommended reading: John Kent,* Elizabeth Fry *(New York: Arco, 1963).*

# COMMANDED *to* PREACH

"*I* will pray once more," said Amanda to herself, "and if there is any such thing as salvation, I am determined to have it this afternoon or die." It was Tuesday, March 17, 1856, and she was ironing. She set the dinner table and, her immediate duties done, she went down to the cellar to pray.

She half expected that her family would find her dead. Had she not prayed before without results? "I cannot remember the time from my earliest childhood that I did not want to be a Christian, and would often pray alone," she wrote. But she could not get the assurance of acceptance from God for which she hungered. She envied the wind and sun and moon, because they were obedient to God, whereas she knew she had often disobeyed. She even asked the sun, moon and wind to carry a message to Jesus that she was a sinner. At another time, she thought that if only she would go to the altar rail at the front of the church, she might achieve peace with God. However, she had determined not to embarrass herself that way. Eventually she became so weary of the ache inside of her that she did go to the altar, but she came away just as miserable as she had been when she went. Satan taunted her that there was no salvation for her. "God does his work quick," she seemed to hear him say.

Amanda was ready to abandon her search for God, but a whisper said, "Pray again." And so she stepped down into the cellar. Once again her prayers seemed futile. She prayed all the things she had prayed before.

## Amanda Smith

**Born:** January 23, 1837, in Long Green, MD
**Education:** Self-educated
**Married:** James Smith around 1863
**Children:** Five
**Died:** February 24, 1915, in Sebring, FL
**Quote:** "Yes, Lord, if You will help me, and give me Your strength, and go with me, I will go."

When the Ku Klux Klan began its activities after the Civil War, Amanda found herself dreading a trip to Knoxville. She told the Lord,

> If being a martyr for Thee would glorify Thee, all right; but then, just to go down there and be butchered by wicked men for their own gratification, without any reference to Thy glory, I'm not willing. And now, Lord, help me. If Thou dost want me to do this, even then, give me the grace and enable me to do it.

This incident just about summarizes Amanda's life and personality—her practicality, her willingness and her chatty intimacy with the Lord.

Darkness settled on her, and she had no relief from the unease that warned her that she was at odds with God.

Finally, in desperation and believing that God would strike her dead because she had promised to get saved or die, she looked up and said, " 'O, Lord, if Thou wilt help me I will believe Thee,' and in the act of telling God I would, I did. O, the peace and joy that flooded my soul!" From that day forward, Amanda had two ambitions in life: to know God better and to tell others about Him.

## Unwise Choices, Growing Wisdom

Born a slave in Maryland in 1837, Amanda was freed when she was three years old. Her father, John Berry, bought himself and his family and moved them to Pennsylvania. He made their home a station on the Underground Railroad, and their property was closely watched to see if they were harboring fugitives. One night a party of slave trackers burst into the Berry home, demanding to know where John was hiding a runaway. The men beat John and tried to stab Amanda's mother. Another time they did catch a terrified fugitive, who leaped from an upstairs window, and they dragged him away in chains. On yet another occasion, one of Amanda's free-born sisters was sold into slavery while she was visiting an aunt in Maryland. Amanda had to borrow $50 to buy her back. Given these experiences, she knew what slavery was all about, so when she experienced the freedom of salvation in Christ, she praised God that she had been freed twice.

Yet Amanda still had to learn obedience. "O, I would God I had always obeyed Him, then would my peace have flowed as the river, but many times I failed."

Two years before her conversion, she had married a man who was kind when he was sober and mean when he was drunk. He went to war and never returned. Because Amanda wanted a share in telling others about God, she next married a deacon who promised to become an evangelist. As it turned out, he was lying to her about his plans, and eventually he abandoned her. She realized that she had not cleared the marriage with the Lord, and her bad choice had serious consequences that followed her through life.

She suffered from poverty and had to work long hours and starve herself so that her children might eat. This suffering taught her to bring every detail of her day to the Lord in prayer. All but one of her children died in infancy, the result of lying in damp rooms while Amanda sweated over laundry to earn money for them. The one daughter who survived to adulthood died in her early twenties.

Amanda's autobiography tells of Christ's faithful dealings with her and Satan's whispers to keep her from obedience. She had her share of fears, doubts and hesitations, but nevertheless she went where God told her to go and clung to Him despite bitter hardships.

## Second Blessing

In the 1860s and afterward, Methodist revivalists urged Christians to experience "the second blessing"—sanctification. This was described as an empowerment of the Holy Spirit that would allow believers to walk in deeper holiness and even to live a perfect life.

John Inskip was a stirring speaker on this theme. One Sunday in 1868, Amanda felt impelled to go hear him preach. She believed Inskip's claim that God could bring every thought and action into subjection to Him, and she asked for this for herself. Waves of joy flooded her soul. Although she was the only black person in the church and afraid of white people, she shouted aloud.

On the way home, she met some very dignified "leading sisters," the kind who looked down on poorer black people, and she was tempted to say nothing to them of her sanctification, but as she drew near, power welled up within her. She knew that she had to be honest about what the Spirit had done for her. "They said, 'Well, Smith, where have you been this morning?'

" 'The Lord,' I said, 'has sanctified my soul.' And they were speechless!"

## Going to the Fair

What does it mean to be "led by the Spirit"? Amanda believed that she had learned. One time around 1869, the Lord instructed her to go to the fair. She questioned this command. It was not her habit to visit such places, but certain that the Holy Spirit was telling her to go, she went, feeling completely out of place. She prayed for direction, and the Lord seemed to tell her where to stand. "I got up and went and stood at the top of the stairs where the people were coming up . . . then came two young men full of glee. The Spirit seemed to pick out one especially, and said, 'Speak to that young man.' " She did, but he respectfully brushed her aside. All that night she felt that she must pray for that young man.

The next day, someone asked Amanda, "Did you hear that Charlie S. is dead?"

"No."

"He was found dead in his bed this morning; he was at the fair the other night well and hearty."

Curiosity prompted Amanda to go look at the dead man. "There he was, dead, no sign of sickness, and the very young man that God had sent me to speak to."

Incidents such as this confirmed to Amanda that in obeying the prompting of her heart, she was obeying God.

## Fiery Letters Commanded Her to Preach

The year after her sanctification, Amanda heard the Lord tell her to preach. This command was followed by a vision in which she saw fiery letters spelling "GO." Women preachers were not yet widely accepted—much less black women. Yet, dressed plainly in black, gray and white, she began speaking in African Methodist Episcopal (AME) churches. Her stirring songs, sung in a rich contralto voice, her vivid testimonies and her obvious faith spurred many others to seek and find a similar joy. The self-educated ex-slave won souls on five continents and challenged many Christians to live lives consistent with what they believed. Through her example, women gained a more prominent role in the AME Church.

## England, India, Africa

In 1878 Amanda was invited to England to hold three months of services. A year later she was still there. From England she went by invitation to India, where she worked for two years. Bishop James M. Thoburn of Bombay wrote,

> I shall never forget one meeting which we were holding in an open square, in the very heart of the city. It was at a time of no little excitement, and some Christian preachers had been roughly handled in the same square a few evenings before. I . . . noticed a great crowd of men and boys, who had succeeded in breaking up a missionary's audience on the other side of the square, rushing towards us with loud cries and

threatening gestures. If left to myself I should have tried to gain the box on which the speakers stood in order to command the crowd, but at the critical moment, our good Sister Smith knelt on the grass and began to pray. As the crowd rushed up to the spot, and saw her beaming face upturned to the evening sky, pouring out her soul in prayer, they became perfectly still, and stood as if transfixed to the spot! Not even a whisper disturbed the solemn silence.

Thoburn said that at a single glance Amanda was able to see through philosophical and religious systems that fooled brilliant men. He asserted that he learned more from her that was of actual value to him as a preacher than from any other person he ever met.

Amanda was gone from the United States for twelve years. Following her successful efforts in India, she worked for eight years as a missionary in Liberia and West Africa, where revival broke out. "The people came from all directions. We went on for two weeks without a break. We had several all-night meetings. . . . Some old men were converted that were never known to pray or be serious before." Amanda did not return to the States until 1890, when malaria, rheumatism and arthritis made it no longer practical for her to labor in Africa. She was fifty-three years old.

> *"Thy will be done." Oh! that word, and to say it from the heart. When you stand by your dear ones dying, with not two dollars for funeral expenses, with a husband and father away, and when he might have come, yet did not, with no one to go to, when the very heavens seemed brass, and the earth iron, and you and your own body exhausted from hard work and watching day and night, and with but little food to sustain the body, then to say, "Thy will be done," from the heart, is more than all burnt offerings and sacrifice; and this prayer, prayed from the heart, is what is meant by being entirely and wholly sanctified.*
>
> *—Amanda Smith*

## No Shelf Life for This Lady

Old age and ill health did not shelve Amanda. After writing her autobiography, which was published in 1893, she opened a home in Chicago for black orphans. To raise support for it, she returned to preaching and singing in churches, both black and white.

She died in 1915 of a paralytic stroke at the age of seventy-eight. Her autobiography, with its homey details of her struggle for survival and hunger for holiness, has become a classic in women's studies.

*Recommended reading: Amanda Smith,* An Autobiography: The Story of the Lord's Dealings with Mrs. Amanda Smith, the Colored Evangelist *(New York: Oxford University Press, 1987).*

# BUILDER *of* WOMEN'S ORGANIZATIONS

"*I'll go sometime, you hear?*" Frances Willard was angry that her brother Oliver was allowed to attend a lecture in town while she had to sit at home with her sister Mary. Why couldn't she go? And why wasn't she allowed to ride a horse? Why could Oliver vote as soon as he came of age, while she could not? Why must she be content to study Shakespeare and the Bible at home while he bent over textbooks in a classroom?

Standing on stumps in Forest Home, Wisconsin, miles from her nearest neighbor, Frances recited speeches to imaginary audiences in rhetoric that was sometimes as angry as the entries in her journal: "*Feel crosser than I have in six months. Had a great time [trouble] with my hair. Mother put it up 'woman fashion.' How I detest the fashion, and the way in which women are obliged to spend their time. Perfectly insipid!*" she wrote. "*I stayed at home as usual and had 'the blues' as usual.*"

One night Frances listened as her father told her mother about the fight for prohibition that was taking place in Maine. "*I wonder if poor, rum-cursed Wisconsin will ever get a law like that,*" he said. Her mother rocked in silence for a while, then said, "*Yes, Josiah, there'll be such a law all over the land some day, when women vote.*" Frances and her mother were to be in complete accord on that opinion.

## Frances Willard

**Born:** Sepember 28, 1739, in Churchville, NY

**Education:** Attended Northwestern Female College

**Married:** Did not marry

**Children:** None

**Died:** February 18, 1898, in New York, NY

**Quote:** "The world is wide, and I will not waste my life in friction when it could be turned into momentum."

## Frying Onions

"Some day, when women vote." In 1857 the vote looked as far off as ever. Even formal educa-

*Dwight L. Moody, world evangelist, was so impressed with Frances Willard that he invited her to become his director of women's ministries, promising her that she could continue her temperance work. She accepted in 1877, but the arrangement lasted for only a year. Frances wanted to include everyone, regardless of denomination, in her work, but Moody needed to remain more doctrinally focused. They parted ways, and Frances continued to reach across barriers whenever she could. Once a number of her followers stormed out when she brought controversial Susan B. Anthony onto the stage with her, but it is a safe bet that Frances would have done it again the next day if she could have.*

tion seemed like an impossible dream for most pioneer girls. The few months of schooling that Frances enjoyed were given to her by her mother, a neighboring preacher, a girl who'd attended a school in the east and an aunt. And there was always the letdown from books when she had to return to the housework she detested. "[W]hen I had to help get dinner one Sunday I fairly cried. To come down to frying onions when I've been away among the rings of Saturn . . ."

Frances was commanded by her father not to fritter away her mind on novels. When Josiah caught her with Charlotte Brontë's *Villette*, he sternly ordered her to put it aside. She did, but inwardly she seethed. In 1857, however, Josiah listened to his daughter's pleas and arranged for her to attend Milwaukee Female College.

After a few delightful months, the plans were changed, and Frances was transferred to Northwestern Female College, a Methodist school in Evanston, Illinois. Her entire family moved there from Forest Home. Northwestern was not then noted for its academic excellence, but it was a college, and Frances seized her opportunity with both hands. Within a month she was at the head of her class, and two years later in 1859 she graduated as valedictorian. Unfortunately, she was unable to give her speech because she had contracted typhoid fever and was in danger of dying.

## "I'll Try to Be a Christian"

For some time Frances had been the subject of intense prayer. The principal of her college described her as an infidel. In a letter to him, Frances stated that she did not wish to go to the altar because she had no feeling for spiritual things. "If there is a God in heaven, a hell, a devil, then I am undone," she said.

But when she contracted the fever and was facing death, Frances made a promise. "If God lets me get well, I'll try to be a Christian girl." When she recovered, she went to the altar, expecting to experience some sudden depth of feeling, but nothing happened. Thirteen more times she went, hoping for a transformation. Baffled, she went home as empty as she had come. And then one night, alone at home, she realized that her conversion was accomplished as soon as she had asked to be saved. She trusted the Scripture that said, "Thou wilt keep him in perfect peace, whose mind is stayed on thee" (Isaiah 26:3), and she experienced no more spiritual concern.

Courtesy Ray Strachey, *Frances Willard* (London: T. Fisher Unwin, 1912)

*Mary Willard, Frances's beloved sister*

## Worthless Days

Once out of school, it must have seemed to Frances that she would never find her niche. Nothing she attempted lasted for long. She kept busy, but she could not see that she did any good and felt that her days were worthless. She confided her unhappiness to her journal and thought she saw a solution. "If I become a teacher in some school that I don't like, and if I go away alone, and try what 'I, myself' can do, and suffer, & am tired and lonely; if I am in a position where I must have all the responsibility . . . if everything is hard for me . . . I think I may grow to be strong and earnest."

In 1860 she accepted a teaching position twenty miles away and developed a missionary zeal to train her pupils in good manners and basic skills. The home in which she stayed was not a Christian home, but she struck up a friendship with Clara, the daughter of the house, and soon taught her to pray. Astonished at the lack of Bible knowledge among the pupils at the school, Frances and Clara started a Sunday school.

## Restless Years

The events of 1861 echoed Frances's own restlessness. Fort Sumpter was fired upon, the first shot of the Civil War, and Frances became engaged and then disengaged to Charles Fowler. Charles had read her diary and made stiff comments about it. He insisted that she read his books of inflexible theology, and once he tested her by pretending that he was going to China as a missionary. The engagement was broken off. Frances wrote that she had liked Charles—until he came to her side of the room.

Her beloved sister Mary died of consumption, and she wrote, "Mary is dead. I write the sentence—stop and look at it—do not know what it means." In memory of her childhood companion, Frances wrote a book titled *Nineteen Beautiful Years.*

Evanston, with its memories of Mary, was unbearable to Frances. She accepted a position in Pittsburgh, Pennsylvania, and for the first time in her life, she attended the opera, the theater and concerts. "I am sure God meant beauty to be enjoyed," she wrote around 1864, after a visit to her father's family, who held narrower views. After Pittsburgh, she taught at various schools but stayed at none of them for very long. She was on her way to another school in 1867 when her father fell ill of tuberculosis. She returned home and nursed him and kept house, which was never an easy task for her.

After Josiah's death, Frances was offered a position as a traveling companion to a wealthy friend, Kate Jackson. To meet her financial needs, she became a foreign correspondent for a Chicago newspaper. The pair spent a delightful two years in Europe. Scandalized by the theaters and shocked by the utter lack of Sunday observance in Paris, Frances wrote, "Kate and I . . . fell to reading our dear neglected Bible to each other this morning and talking of the only things that last." They both longed for home.

Once home, Frances immediately became the first woman president of a college when she was given the leadership of newly organized Evanston College, which was under the oversight of Northwestern University. She had to collect money, build new facilities and recruit students, and she succeeded on all counts. One of her students explained why: "She was always planning for our happiness and welfare, and would go to any amount of trouble to gratify us. " Unfortunately, the man to whom Frances had earlier been engaged became the head of Northwestern in 1872, and he harassed her until she felt compelled to resign from Evanston in June of 1874.

As a girl, Frances had practiced speaking from a stump. Following her resignation from Northwestern, she spoke at a missionary meeting, and a businessman in attendance was so impressed with her address that he offered her $50 and the best audience in Chicago for her to lecture on any topic she chose. After some hesitation, she agreed and so captured her audience that she was offered 200 speaking engagements within 2 weeks.

## On Her Way to History

Alcoholism was rampant in the post-Civil War United States. Drunkenness soaked up money that should have gone for food and rent, and wives suffered when their husbands became violent from the drink. Because of this, women began to demand the prohibition of liquor. In 1873 the Women's Christian Temperance Union (WCTU) was born when women spontaneously gathered to pray and demonstrate in front of saloons. The following year, Frances knelt and prayed in public at a Pittsburgh WCTU rally. At once her speaking engagements fell off, and some were canceled.

Within a week, however, she was offered the presidency of the Chicago WCTU. Uncertain whether to accept the position, Frances prayed and turned to the Scriptures. Psalm 37:3 leaped out at her: "Trust in the LORD, and do good; so shalt thou dwell in the land, and verily thou shalt be fed." She accepted the job, without pay (her mother agreed to this, although she was dependent on Frances for her livelihood), and Frances was on her way to the history books.

The rest of Frances's life was spent working with the Women's Christian Temperance Union. In the early years, fainting from hunger and walking because she hadn't a nickel for the tram, she threw herself heart and soul into the endeavor. For years, she supported her mother and her secretary with only her lecture fees. Her zeal sustained her for a time, but at last she fell ill. It was not until 1866, when her friends learned that she was destitute, that she was provided with a salary.

Frances eventually became secretary to the national temperance movement and then its president in 1879. Arguing that the temperance movement could not succeed unless women were allowed to vote, Frances marshaled the women of the temperance movement behind the battle for suffrage. She was reelected to the presidency of the movement,

*But I think the greatest evidence of how deeply she [Frances] was rooted in Christianity was her power of forgiveness. I know no one who felt more acutely the bitterness of ingratitude, the heartache of a slight, or the stab of an enemy. I have seen her lip quiver as she read a letter, and her hand tremble, and I have realized how profoundly the human pain and disappointment entered her soul, and yet after a moment's struggle, she would set herself to devise some way by which she could go out of the routine of her life, and, by giving herself some extra trouble, write the word or do the act that would make the one who had injured her feel that all was right, that love could never fail.*

*—Lady Henry Somerset*

and by all accounts, she was successful with her work because she accepted women as they were. She turned enemies into friends by speaking the best of them and expecting kindness

Courtesy Anna A. Gordon, *The Beautiful Life of Frances Willard* (Chicago: WCTU, 1898)

*The first schoolhouse where Frances taught*

and cooperation from them. In her view, people—even her enemies—were essentially good.

Frances always was concerned with more than temperance. After all, it was but one of many women's issues. She continually fought to have the temperance union spread itself like a blanket over all women's issues, and to some extent, she succeeded. The Union got temperance education added to school curriculums and exerted pressure for prison reform, anti-prostitution laws and the right of women to vote.

In 1890 Frances's mother died, and after that, Frances was restless. Her health failed, in large measure due to overwork, and she died just eight years later of grippe and chronic anemia. Her last words were, "How good it is to be with God."

In 1905 Frances became the first woman to be honored with a statue in Washington, DC. In a joint resolution, Congress recognized her as one of the most eminent women in American history. Many women's groups of America today can claim her as the mother of their tactics and interests.

*Recommended reading: Anna Adams Gordon and Lady Henry Somerset,* The Beautiful Life of Frances E. Willard *(Chicago: WCTU, 1898).*

# Part 8
## Mothering the World

*They mothered
many into the
kingdom of God.*

# "I JUST ACTED *like* a MOTHER"

*W*hen the French government wanted to transport ex-slaves to Mana, French Guiana, under guard and in chains, Anne-Marie Javouhey refused. They would travel un-chained and accompanied by a single nun, she said. When she was asked how she managed to tame the tough characters of French Guiana and Devil's Island, she replied, "I just acted like a mother among her children."

A mother, maybe, but a tough one. As King Louis-Philippe sent Anne-Marie off to Guiana, he said, "Take my word for it, my friends. Madame Javouhey is a great man."

## Anne-Marie Javouhey

**Born:** November 10, 1779, in Chamblanc, France

**Education:** Unknown

**Married:** Did not marry

**Children:** None

**Died:** July 15, 1851, in Paris, France

**Quote:** "May God be glorified! In everything and everywhere may his Holy Will be done!"

## Girl Hero

Anne-Marie, or "Nanette," as she was called, was born in Chamblanc, France, in 1779, the fifth of ten children. Even as a small girl, she was devout. When she was praying in the village church one day, she heard a voice within her saying, "You will belong to Me. You will be consecrated to Me. You will serve the poor and care for orphans." Nanette took the promise seriously.

When she was ten years old, the French Revolution was already drenching French soil with blood. The atheistic leaders of the Revolution hated the Roman Catholic Church, and they shut down monasteries and confiscated church property. Priests were ordered to take a pledge of allegiance to the secular government, a pledge that superseded their religious vows. Any who did not

177

Anne-Marie Javouhey was beatified by the Roman Catholic Church on October 15, 1850. It was a fitting tribute, as the renewal of French missions in Africa can be attributed to her. She had such a way of winning loyalty that when the people of Mana, French Guiana, were told to elect a deputy to parliament, they chose her. When they were told that a woman could not assume the seat, they refused to vote at all.

were considered traitors and were subject to death. The priests traveled across France in secret, holding services for faithful believers.

By the time Nanette had entered her teens, she was adept at hiding faithful priests and gathering trustworthy peasants who wanted to meet for worship. When the worship was over, she would lead the fugitive clergymen onward to their next underground contact. The authorities suspected that Nanette was the one who was helping priests slip across the river Saone, but even those radicals did not care to arrest a heroic thirteen-year-old girl.

One of the brave priests, Abbé Ballanche, encouraged Nanette to become a nun. At a mass that was celebrated secretly in her house in 1798, she took a vow of celibacy and promised to devote her life to the education of children and to helping the poor. When a Revolutionary mob set fire to the Chamblanc chapel, Nanette dashed into the flames and ran out, clutching the monstrance and the holy vessels that she had rescued.

Master Balthazar Javouhey wanted his daughter to settle down, marry, have children and manage the family farms. He thought that she would do a better job of it than his sons would. He encouraged a likely young man to woo his daughter, but instead Nanette talked the boy into becoming a Trappist monk. She also talked her two brothers into becoming churchmen.

When Chamblanc's priest returned after the Revolution had quieted somewhat, he was astonished to see what Nanette and her sisters had accomplished while he was gone, training the villagers in the catechism. He recommended to Balthazar that Nanette be allowed to enter a convent.

She lived for a year with the Sisters of Charity at Basancon, but the quiet life did not satisfy her. While meditating and praying for guidance, Nanette had a vision. She saw herself surrounded by men with black skin, all of whom were holding their arms out to her. A voice informed her that these were the children who had been given to her and that she was to found a new order within the Church.

Nanette was not sure what the message meant. Throughout the year of 1803, she tried to work with the Cistercians in Switzerland, establishing small peasant communities among them, but she found that it too was not her calling. Finally, she returned to Chamblanc and opened a school in 1806.

## Grape-Picker's Dress

In 1805 Pope Pius VII had stopped in Chalon-sur-Saône to celebrate Easter. Four peasant girls—the Javouhey sisters—from the village of Chamblanc attended that special mass, taking the bread from the pope's own hands. Then they waited in the hope of receiving a summons. The Javouhey sisters had dared to ask for a private audience with the pope.

Courtesy Aotrou Madec, *Leanez santel Anna-Mari Javouhey hag urz sant Joseph a Cluny* (Moullerez ar C'haourrier du Finistere, 1920)

**Nanette teaching**

Though he was busy, the pope saw them. In a kindly manner, he asked them questions, and he blessed them, encouraging them to keep up their good work. Two years later, Nanette, her sisters and five others formed a new order: the Religious Society of St. Joseph, better known as the Congregation of St. Joseph of Cluny. They donned blue-and-black habits that were designed to mimic a grape-picker's dress.

The order's educational methods were influenced by the Lancasterian system, which relied on drills and rote memory and used advanced students as monitors for laggards. When the order opened a school in Paris, it attracted favorable comment and the governor of Réunion Island asked Nanette to send some sisters to open a school for black students. In response, Nanette sent out her first missionaries in 1817.

## Nanette Masters Africa and Guiana

France controlled Senegal at the time, and the success of the sisters in Réunion convinced Senegal to call for their assistance. Nanette herself went, and there she renovated the hospital. Disgusted by the assumption of white superiority, she decreed that all people would be treated as equals on her premises. She began a program to train native clergy to spread the gospel to their own people, and she even started agricultural communities where she could impose moral order.

Having seen her ability to organize a large plantation in Senegal, the French government asked Nanette to straighten up the Mana district in Guiana, South America. The men who had been sent to do the job had failed.

*I have been thinking about our lives together these past forty-five years and I am amazed by God's generosity to us. We have been very blessed. It is a great reward for obedience—all that we have been permitted to do. Always follow the Holy Will of God.*
—Anne-Marie Javouhey

Nanette sailed for Guiana on June 26, 1828, at the head of an expedition consisting of 100 persons. For four years she struggled against petty local jealousies, snakes, swarming insects and ceaseless rains. Over time, a church arose. Formerly villainous men attended nightly prayer meetings, and a new dock began to receive ships. Livestock grazed in well-fenced pastures, and plantations that raised bananas and manioc emerged from the jungle. But the government of France changed in 1830, and the experiment faltered for lack of support. Nanette returned to France in 1833.

## A King's Call for Help

At the time, there was a worldwide movement that was clamoring against slavery, and King Louis Philippe indicated that he intended to free many of the slaves in Guiana. This raised howls from the colonists, who wanted to keep men as beasts of burden and tillers of their crops and who feared the strength of liberated black men. They swore that black people did not have the mental capability to manage their own affairs outside of Africa. So loud were these outcries that the king became alarmed. He knew full well that slave owners would make it as difficult as possible for freed slaves to succeed.

Five hundred slaves walked off of farms in Guiana and proceeded to the capital city of Cayenne. Without jobs and penniless, they became a serious public burden, and the king determined to free them. He summoned Nanette and asked her if the slaves were really incapable of caring for themselves outside of Africa. Nonsense, said Nanette. The king asked her if she would return to French Guiana to help establish and civilize the 500 slaves in Mana. After much prayer, she said that she would try. As she left the palace in 1835, the king himself accompanied her to her carriage, where he called her a "great man."

## Greed and Jealousy Hinder

Many eyes were turned on Nanette as she mapped out the colony's structure so that it resembled a religious community. Signs of success soon became apparent as new villages emerged.

Nanette still faced challenges, however. On one occasion slave owners who opposed emancipation bribed a black man to upset Nanette's boat and drown her. Although she was forewarned of the danger, Nanette went aboard anyway, and consequently, nothing happened. But her enemies could and did hinder supplies from reaching her, and they arrested her associates who visited Cayenne on business.

A second front of attack developed when Bishop d'Héricourt of Autun, an ex-cavalryman, claimed that Nanette's order was within his jurisdiction and determined to exert control over the Congregation of St. Joseph of Cluny. He tried to force the nuns to rewrite their constitution to give him more authority over them. Nanette refused. Consequently, the bishop prevailed upon the Apostolic Prefect of Guinea to deny her the sacraments. For two years Nanette was not allowed to approach the communion table. "We must pray for him as a benefactor," she said in response, "for he has given us the opportunity to suffer."

*Nanette denied her body in order to make herself useful—though she was always seasick, she was nonetheless a tireless traveler. Altogether she traveled over 75,000 miles—40,000 by land and 35,000 by sea. "I am no more afraid of the sea and its sickness than I am of the land," she asserted.*

Despite these hindrances, the slaves were freed on May 21, 1838, and each freed family found themselves to be the proud possessors of a cottage and a sum of money with which they could begin a new life. It was ultimately Nanette's uncompromising determination that brought this to pass. In time, government inspectors rated Mana as more orderly and prosperous than Cayenne itself.

## As It Should Be

In 1843 Nanette sailed back to France. As she boarded the ship, the priest who was on board refused to give her communion. "Very well," she said, "but if anything goes wrong, you will answer to God for it."

Once she was home again, Nanette faced the continued opposition of d'Héricourt, but she was eventually able to establish a working relationship with him. She rejoiced to open new work in India, Tahiti and South America. Her congregation increased to 118 houses and over 1,000 sisters.

In March of 1851 Nanette suffered a stroke and went into a coma. On June 8 she sank very low, and everyone thought that she would die that night. Bishop d'Héricourt died that same day, but Nanette recovered a little.

A few days later, when she was told that the bishop had died, she said, "We almost met, he and I, on that very day, before the judgment seat of God. So he's gone in ahead of me, that good bishop. Well, that is as it should be. A bishop should always enter first."

On July 14 Nanette prayed for the bishop's soul one last time and then slipped into eternity the following morning.

*Recommended reading: Henri Daniel-Rops,* The Heroes of God: Eleven Courageous Men and Women Who Risked Everything to Spread the Catholic Faith *(Garden City, NY: Doubleday, 1959).*

# "SHE'S GAME"

Courtesy W.P. Livingstone, *Mary Slessor of Calabar* (London: Hodder and Stoughton, 1917)

*W*ith drums pounding a rhythm for the oarsmen, the canoe pushed off from the shore and into a blinding rain. The oarsmen dipped their paddles into the water and drove the hand-carved log up the Calabar River. Under a shack that sat on the canoe, Mary Slessor sat with five black children huddling around her.

Early that morning, Mary had hustled boxes and baskets down to the river, but the canoe that was supposed to take her to begin her new work in Okoyong did not appear. She began to lose her confidence. Twelve years in Africa had shown her how hard it is to change people's ways. The more she thought about it, the more overwhelming her job looked.

Fortunately, the canoe arrived before Mary could change her mind. King Eyo came to see her off, and, realizing that she was nervous, he calmed her fears by promising that he would keep in close touch with her by canoe. Mary thanked him and took her place onboard with the babies whose lives she had saved. Another great adventure with God was about to begin.

## Dreams of the Mission Field

Mary had long dreamed of that day. When she was just a child, her mother taught her about Calabar, the deadly coast of Nigeria that was known as "the white man's grave." Like other Scottish children, Mary donated her precious pennies to help the mission work, and eventually she asked the Presbyterian Church to send her to Calabar too.

## Mary Slessor

**Born:** December 2, 1848, near Aberdeen, Scotland
**Education:** Sporadic education
**Married:** Did not marry
**Children:** None
**Died:** January 13, 1915, in the Calabar region of Nigeria
**Quote:** *"God and one are always a majority."*

*Bitten by a poisonous snake while walking, she sucked the poison from her own finger. When one of her babies was snatched by a leopard, she rushed at it with a firebrand. In the dark of a tiger-infested jungle, she sang to comfort her children. Years after her death, African women still reenacted the story of the time she drove off a hippopotamus by yelling and waving her umbrella at it. Such was the courage and faith of Mary Slessor.*

In 1875 her answer came in the mail. "Dear Miss Slessor, I take great pleasure in informing you that the Board of Foreign Missions accepts your offer to serve as a missionary, and you have been appointed teacher to Calabar." The twenty-seven-year-old factory worker, who rejoiced to read those words, had never before set foot outside of Scotland.

## Wee and Thin

Born in a suburb of Aberdeen, Scotland, Mary knew extreme poverty as a child. Her shoemaker father spent most of his wages on drink. The family moved to Dundee when Mary was ten years old, and when she was eleven she was sent to work in the sweatshops of Dundee as a common mill hand, preparing jute and flax for the weavers. In time she became a skilled weaver who was able to manage two sixty-inch looms at once, turning out ships' canvas, sacking, sheets and cloth.

As a young girl, she was exhausted by her work, for she was, in her own words, "wee and thin and not very strong," but Mary still made the most of her opportunities. She attended school when she was not working, and there she learned reading, writing, arithmetic, geography, sewing, knitting and a little music. If she was too tired to follow the arithmetic problems, the teacher punished her by making her stand up during class. In the winter, when the sky grew dark early, she had to dodge drunks and thieves as she walked home in the dark to do her chores and face her drunken father.

Robert Slessor was an alcoholic, and when he came home violent from drinking, red-haired Mary always stood up to him. To protect her from beatings, Mary's mother shooed her out into the street, where she would wander, crying, until her father fell into a drunken sleep.

Mary was quick with her tongue. She described herself as a "reckless lassie" full of mischief, who ran barefoot, jumped and climbed trees like a boy. She would never com-

pletely outgrow her tomboy practices or her temper. One of Mary's brothers teased her about her
red hair by calling her "carrots" and "fire."

Courtesy W.P. Livingstone, *Mary
Slessor of Calabar* (London: Hodder
and Stoughton, 1917)

## Forgiveness in Dying Days

One day an old widow gathered Mary and some
other young children around her hearth. Pointing
to the fire blazing in it, she warned them that unless they repented and believed in Christ, their
souls would "burn in the lowin' bleezin' fire for
ever and ever!" The words frightened Mary and
she became a Christian.

*Mary holds court.*

Sunday was a day of happiness for Mary, because there was no work. Going to church, with its
organ music, wonderful hymns and missionary
letters that told of distant lands, was the highlight of her week.

After she became a Christian, Mary tried to help children whose lives were as bleak as
her own had been. She held Bible classes to tell them of the friend she had found in
Christ Jesus. She took classes of boys into the countryside for picnics and raced with
them. Unfortunately, her behavior raised the eyebrows of people in the pews who always wanted things to be done "properly."

Some boys did not want to hear what Mary had to say. They jeered and slung mud at
her. One time they surrounded her while their leader whirled a lead weight around and
around on a string, approaching closer and closer to her face. She stood without flinch-
ing, praying inwardly but determined not to duck or run. The leader grazed her fore-
head with the weight, but she stood with steady eyes. Finally, the boy dropped the
weight. "It's OK, boys," he said. "She's game!" He made his whole gang attend Mary's
Bible meeting that night.

Another time, a boy became a Christian when Mary offered to accept a flogging if
only he would attend Bible meetings. Through her hard work, she led many youngsters
to Christ.

## In the "White Man's Graveyard"

On August 5, 1876, Mary sailed for Africa aboard the S.S. *Ethiopia* on her way to
Calabar in Nigeria. She would need all of her pluck where she was going. If anyone
asked her why she was leaving her missionary work in Scotland, where there were many

Courtesy W.P. Livingstone, *Mary Slessor of Calabar* (London: Hodder and Stoughton, 1917)

### Mary's well-worn Bible

people who did not know Christ, she had an answer: In Scotland, no one grew up far from the sight of a church spire. In Africa, millions had never so much as heard that there was a Church.

In Calabar, Mary lived in Duke Town with a well-established missionary couple, the Andersons. Her main responsibility was to work in the mission school, and she quickly learned Efik, the local language. Mary was absentminded and often came late to meals. Mrs. Anderson said that Mary had to do without dinner if she was late, but she still lost track of time. Sometimes "Daddy" Anderson brought food up to her room.

Mary soon learned about cruel gods that were carved of wood and stone and to whom the Nigerians sacrificed humans. She put her own life on the line trying to rescue slaves and women from death. She also fought against the practice of judging by ordeal, which meant that a person who was suspected of doing wrong might be forced to eat poisoned beans, or boiling oil might be poured over him. The gods were supposed to protect the innocent from harm, but of course they didn't. Everyone tested by these methods was "guilty." Such cruelty infuriated Mary. When one man poured boiling oil on the hands of an eleven-year-old boy, Mary grabbed a scoop of the scalding liquid and chased the man to pour it on him and show him that he was not innocent either. Everyone laughed, except the poor boy, who was still screaming in agony.

Another horror that Mary discovered was the treatment of wives after the deaths of their husbands. They were automatically suspected of witchcraft, and a chicken was beheaded in front of each wife. Depending on how the head flopped, the wife was pronounced either guilty or innocent. The legs of the "guilty" wives were broken, and the women were thrown alive into their husband's graves. Ma Eme, a chief's sister who went through this ordeal, fainted from relief when her chicken declared her innocent. After that, she often informed Mary secretly when ordeals were happening so that Mary could rescue the accused women.

The Nigerians also enslaved and branded each other, and girls were fattened up to sell as slave wives. Slaves were expendable, and when a chief died, dozens of his slaves were killed. Other evils included throwing unwanted babies into the bush to be nibbled by insects or gobbled by leopards. Twins were believed to be a great evil. The Nigerians

believed that one of the two had the devil as its father, but since no one knew which one it was, both
were buried alive or thrown into the forest. Their
mother was driven away to die.

The tribes fought and danced and got drunk.
Sometimes they killed and ate one another. Everyone lived in fear. A secret society known as the
Egbo went around in masks and beat people. One
time Mary chased a group of Egbo and tore off a
mask, exposing the sheepish face of the man who
was wearing it.

Malaria weakened Mary, however, and she had to
return to Scotland in 1879. While she was on furlough, she told church women about Calabar, and
many of them became interested in her work.
Strangely, although Mary was very bold when she
was talking to African chiefs, she was too shy to
speak in front of white men in Scotland's churches.

> *God help those poor helpless women. They are treated worse than animals. Today I had a crowd of people. How wicked they were! I have had a murder, a poison bean case, a suicide, a man branding his slave wife all over her face and body, a man with a gun who shot four people. It is all horrible.*
> *—Mary Slessor*

## Climbing Trees in Old Town

When she returned to Africa late in 1880, Mary was allowed to work alone in Old
Town. She liked her new freedom. For fun, she climbed trees. She ate when she felt like
it, and she set her own work pace. Her house was soon full of orphans and twins whom
she rescued, fed and cuddled.

One twin became so sick that Mary took her and the other babies into the hills where
it was cooler. A leopard entered Mary's tent and seized a baby boy in its mouth. Mary
grabbed a flaming stick and drove it into the leopard's face. The leopard dropped the
boy and fled, howling. Fortunately, the baby was not hurt.

While at Old Town, Mary ate African food and learned African ways. She learned to cure
sickness with simple medicines. When trade routes were cut off by a war, she secretly led
men across the mission station at night so that they could sell their goods. When Chief
Okon asked her to visit Ibaka and teach his people about Christ, King Eyo sent her up the
river in an impressive war canoe with thirty-three oarsmen. Mary decided that she wanted
to work in Okoyong, but the mission board would not let her go there.

Again Mary became ill and had to return to Scotland in 1883. When she recovered,
she could not go directly back to Africa because her sister was dying. The last three

Courtesy W.P. Livingstone, *Mary Slessor of Calabar* (London: Hodder and Stoughton, 1917)

*Mary with some of her orphan children*

members of Mary's family died within a year of one another, and it was almost two years before she was able to return to Africa.

## Courage Is Faith Conquering Fear

More than ever, Mary wanted to work "up-country," or farther inland. The mission board was still afraid to send her alone, and other missionaries did not like to work with Mary because she lived a helter-skelter life. Mary's style was so much a part of her that she couldn't change. She also knew that she needed to work alone so that she would always be ready to drop everything at a moment's notice to help where she was needed or she would never save lives.

Finally, the mission gave in. On August 4, 1888, Mary set out for Okoyong with her adopted children in tow. The canoe landed near dusk. An eerie silence hung over the forest, and no one came to meet her. It turned out that everyone was attending a funeral. Mary had to find her way to a hut in the darkness and pouring rain. To calm her children's fear of leopards, she sang silly songs. "What is courage, but faith conquering fear?" she asked.

From then on, Mary worked alone, pushing farther and farther inland. Because she understood African customs so well, villagers brought their quarrels to her to settle. The British government made her a vice-consul with authority to judge.

As the slave trade wound down, the people of the countryside needed a new source of income, and Mary helped them make peace with the people on the coast so that they could trade palm oil in exchange for goods. Her real contribution, however, was in bringing an end to certain wicked ways among the villagers. She grabbed women and took them to her house before they could be forced to drink poison. More than once she sat up all night, or even for several nights, to protect slaves from execution. Gradually it dawned on the Africans that lives were worth saving.

Mary loved her people so much that when the mission board would not allow her to move into the Emyong area, she gave up her year of furlough to work there. She was fifty-five when she moved to Itu, the former stronghold of slavery.

When the administration built roads around Itu, Mary learned to ride a bicycle so that she could double her usefulness, and she built stations farther into the bush. The mission board ordered her to go back to Okoyong, but she refused. By that time, she considered herself to be the feet of the Church and saw that the most desperate need was far upriver. The mission gave in.

Sick and exhausted, Mary continued to drive herself to build, teach and administer justice. She boxed the ears of those whom she caught lying in court.

In 1914 Mary fell so ill that she was taken by canoe to the government hospital at Use. She recovered for a few weeks but collapsed again in January. As she lay semiconscious, she whispered in Efik, the language that had become her own, "*O Abasi, sana mi yok.*" "O God, release me."

She died on January 13, 1915, having ended many evil tribal practices and having been an influence for good over thousands of square miles of Africa.

*Recommended reading: Carol Christian and Gladys Plummer,* God and One Redhead: Mary Slessor of Calabar *(London: Hodder and Stoughton, 1970).*

# MOTHER
## *to*
# IMMIGRANTS

*I*ndignantly, *Caroline Chisholm viewed the filthy room, which was only fourteen-by-fourteen feet square. Her appeals had finally persuaded the Australian government to allot a little space to her. But why had such a trifle been so stubbornly denied to her for so long? She didn't stay angry for long, however. At least she now had a place to carry on her work.* "I determined on trusting to Providence to increase its size, and prove my usefulness," *she wrote.*

*She decided that she must begin by sleeping in the room that night.* "I retired wearied to rest. But I was put to the proof at starting: scarce was the light out, when I fancied a few dogs must be in the room, and, in some terror, I got a light." *To her horror, she saw rats in every direction.* "My first act was to throw on my cloak, and get at the door with the intent to leave the building."

*She hesitated, however. If she ran, she would be the laughingstock of the town, and her plan to shelter immigrant girls would be ruined.*

> I therefore lighted a second candle, and seating myself on the bed, kept there until three rats, descending from the roof, alighted on my shoulders. I knew that I was getting into a fever, in fact, that I should be very ill before morning; but to be out-generalled by

## Caroline Chisholm

**Born:** May 30, 1808, in Northhamptonshire, England

**Education:** Studied with her cousins' governess

**Married:** Archibald Chisholm in 1830

**Children:** Nine

**Died:** March 25, 1877, in Fulham, England

**Quote:** "I was impressed with the idea, that God had, in a particular manner, fitted me for this work."

*For more than twenty years, Caroline Chisholm's portrait appeared on the Australian $5 bill. She deserved that honor, for she gave hope to thousands of Australians. One of the secrets of Caroline's success was careful attention to detail; she worked hard and came prepared. A deeper secret was that she obeyed the inner prompting of God.*

*rats was too much. I got up with some resolution; I had two loaves and some butter (for my office, bedroom, and pantry were one); I cut it into slices, placed the whole in the middle of the room, put a dish of water convenient, and with a light by my side, I kept my seat on the bed, reading "Abercrombie," and watching the rats until four in the morning.*

At one point Caroline counted thirteen rats at the dish. "The following night I gave them a similar treat, with addition of arsenic," she wrote.

## Treated like Trollops

Only a desperate need could have led Caroline to closet herself with rats, and that need was the plight of immigrant girls who were arriving in Australia in the late 1830s and early 1840s. These young women were orphans, slum children or asylum inmates, sent to the colonies by the government—and not necessarily arriving in Australia by their own free will. They were told that they must leave the ship within ten days after their arrival, whether they had jobs or not.

A newcomer to Australia herself, Caroline first learned of the girls' plight in 1839 when she saw a group of them standing confused and dejected on the shore. She spoke with them and learned that they were sleeping at night in the shelter of "the rocks," Sydney's crime district, with their pathetic bundles of belongings beside them.

No one would hire them. Although most of them were decent girls—it wasn't their fault that they were orphans—they were branded by society as trollops. Part of the problem was that most of them were Irish, and the Protestants of Sydney despised the girls' Catholic faith. Other problems were that criminals who had been put on the ships in the past had given a bad name to others who were sent to Australia, and some of the girls had turned to prostitution when their hunger became unbearable. Caroline found the girls unwilling to speak of their pasts. The long voyage that had ended in rejection and hunger "seemed to have cut their lives in two."

## Motives of Love

Caroline Jones was born in 1808 in England into a family of solid farmers. Like her mother, she was a redhead. Her father, William, was notable for his generosity and kindness.

One day as the family sat down to dinner, they heard a commotion in the village. William went out to learn the cause of the disturbance and found the villagers pelting an old Roman Catholic priest with mud and stones. William, who was respected in the town, ordered a halt to the persecution and took the old fellow home to clean and feed him.

Five-year-old Caroline asked the priest all sorts of questions, and in slow English he told her about France and other lands. The abbé had fled

Courtesy National Library of Australia

*Sketch of an immigrant home built to Carolyn's specifications*

to England during the French Revolution. Later, Caroline converted to the Catholic religion, and it may be that the seeds of her conversion were planted in those days when the kind old man repaid his benefactors by entertaining their daughter. William, who was past sixty when Caroline was born, died before she turned six.

Caroline was twenty-two when she married handsome Archibald Chisholm in 1830. The marriage had not been a foregone conclusion. For years Caroline had dreamed of achieving some good in the world. Even as a child she had sailed her own little ship full of immigrants across a washtub to Australia, making it return with loads of wheat. It was in her blood to help others. As well as helping villagers and old priests, her family had fed wounded veterans of the Napoleonic wars who came to their door. Caroline felt that she would betray herself if she did not continue this tradition, and she told Archy so.

If she agreed to marry him, she said, he must agree absolutely to support her in whatever good service she undertook. He would never change her, she said, and she would never be content to act the part of a conventional officer's wife. Archy insisted that he understood, but Caroline gave him a month to think it over. It was a month in which she refused to see him. If he did not come back, she would understand. Thirty-one days later, Archy was back.

Archy was assigned to Madras, India, in 1832, and Caroline moved there with him. In the fort where they lived, the society was comfortable. In Black Town, however, Caroline noticed that the children of poorer soldiers were neglected. Orphans might be sold, and other girls either were married young or became soldiers' women.

Courtesy Harold Cazneux, National
Library of Australia

*"The Rocks" in Sydney.
With nowhere else to go,
single girls off the ship
huddled in this tough
neighborhood.*

Caroline began a school for the girls. Although it was not "proper," she asked Archy to move to Black Town where she could personally supervise the school. Remembering his promise, he agreed.

Caroline laid out a very practical course for the students, which included housekeeping, market buying and cooking, as well as the "three R's." She came to the conclusion that only love was reliable enough to act as a consistent motivator for her students, so she determined to encourage them with love and to teach the girls to commit themselves to their tasks from love toward their siblings, their parents and others. She used the rod sparingly.

While in India, Caroline bore the first of her own nine children. By 1837 Archy had completed seven years of service and was due for furlough. Rather than return to England or his native Scotland, the Chisolms decided to take a look at Australia. Caroline found it hard to give up her school, but she had established it well and its continued success seemed assured. After a trouble-filled seven-month voyage, they reached Sydney, where the work with the immigrant girls was opened up to her.

## Divided Lives

Moved with sympathy, Caroline found out what each girl was able to do and promised to help them. At once she called on her acquaintances and was able to place several of the girls as servants in Australian homes. Those whom Caroline couldn't place she took home with her. Her housekeeper, babysitter and friend, Miss Galvin, taught the girls a few household skills, and soon Caroline had placed them all. Of course, that took care of only one batch of girls. Ships loaded with more girls were arriving regularly.

Shocked by Sydney's neglect of the young women, Caroline studied the immigration problem. She continued to help the girls as they arrived, writing letters to place some and taking others home with her. She saw that many of them would be employable if they were taught a few skills, and she considered opening a school of domestic industry. But, when she consulted Archy, he thought that she could do more. "I think the whole of migration will be your field," he said.

The Chisholms eventually returned to Windsor, New South Wales. Archy was recalled to active duty and sailed away. A letter from an immigrant girl took Caroline to Sydney again, and there she found more shocking conditions. She could not harden her heart. "From this period, I devoted all my leisure time in endeavoring to serve these poor girls, and felt determined with God's blessing, never to rest until decent protection was afforded them." The work was painful to Caroline, for it meant that she had to increasingly leave her own children in the care of others. But, stopgap measures were no longer sufficient. To quiet her conscience, she knew she must throw herself fully into the task.

## An Appeal to the Governor

Learning that an old barracks was empty except for some stores, Caroline appealed to the governor, Sir George Gipps, in 1841 for its use as a shelter for newly arrived girls. The governor eventually agreed to meet with her. He expected to see an old lady in a cap and spectacles who would talk to him about his soul, but he was "amazed when my aide introduced a handsome stately young woman who proceeded to reason the question as if she thought her reason and experience too, worth as much as mine." All the same, the governor's answer was "no." Caroline persisted in her appeals, but the governor continued to reject her pleas. He told her that she overrated the powers of her mind.

Meanwhile, Caroline established a job registry and managed to win permission to "frank," or mail without postal charge, a survey to the interior of Australia for the purpose of learning what jobs would be available to her girls, what they paid, how best to transport the young women to the settlements and so forth. She gathered her information from common men.

The governor hastily called Caroline into his office. "Mrs. Chisholm! when I gave you the privilege of franking, I presumed you would address yourself to the magistrates, the clergy, and the principle [sic] settlers; but who pray are these John Vardys and Dick Hogans and other people of whom I have never heard since I have been in the colony?"

Caroline stated flatly that the "respectable" men would have had to go to their overseers to get the information and then would have answered her questions vaguely. "I want to know, as nearly as possible, what numbers of laborers each district can absorb and of what class and at what wages." She urged the governor to wait for the survey results, certain that he would see that she had asked exactly the right people. The governor was appeased.

## Suffering Brings Results

Despite Caroline's efforts, the problem did not go away. Hundreds of girls continued to arrive off of the ships with nowhere to go and no food to eat. One girl, Mary Teague, was

Courtesy Reserve Bank of Australia

*Caroline on the Australian
$5 bill*

seen staggering down a road. Charged with drunkenness, she protested to the court that she was just wobbly from hunger, not having had a bite to eat in two days. The judge did not believe her and ordered her to be exposed in the stocks for an hour. When she was released, she wandered off until she collapsed. She was found lying in a ditch, almost dead, with nothing but the clothes on her back. *The Chronicle*, a local newspaper, printed the story on September 11, 1841, with a number of sorry details.

The governor finally folded and said that Caroline could have a bit of the barracks in which to house the girls. But, he told her that she must not count on the government for a penny of the costs. As slender as his concession was, it made Caroline happy. Well-wishers had already promised their financial assistance, and she set out to collect the funds. But, to her dismay, one after another of the well-wishers waffled. A priest from her own church refused to back her plan. "I felt a dreariness of spirit creep over me and confirmed, in my opinion, that to leave Sydney for a few days would be prudent."

On her way to catch the steamer to Parramatta, Caroline met Flora, a young woman with whom she'd spoken before. Flora had been drinking rum and became insolent with Caroline. The intuitive Caroline sensed that the young woman was contemplating suicide and insisted on accompanying her. Flora was reluctant, but with tender questions, Caroline drew Flora's story out. The man Flora had taken up with had abandoned her, and, learning of her disgrace, Flora's brother had disowned her. She pointed to the spot where she meant to drown herself.

After making Flora promise not to kill herself, Caroline found a room for the unhappy girl. She saw this "chance" meeting with Flora as an example of "Special Providence," and it put a new boldness in her. "From this time I never thought of human help," she said.

Immediately after this incident, Rev. Stiles of the Church of England, while frankly admitting that he doubted Caroline's word and distrusted her Catholic influence, said that her project was a worthy one and that he would support it if she could overcome his objections. Caroline did. Rev. Stiles made a contribution and was imitated by several other Church of England clergy. From then on, the work was funded, and Caroline proved that trust in her was merited.

A few days after her experience with the rats, Caroline obtained more space in the barracks and was soon sheltering ninety girls. Her principal duty, it seemed, was to expel men, who entered one door as quickly as she shooed them out another. To protect the reputations of the girls, she continued to spend her nights with them in the barracks, away from her own children. This distressful separation lasted for a year.

In that one year alone, Caroline assisted over 1,000 immigrant girls. She herself helped them find employment as servants in homes and inns. She drew up a simple contract form to protect the girls she helped, and her registry became quite efficient.

Changes in the immigration system eventually improved the situation enough that Caroline was able to return to her family in 1842, but she remained deeply involved with the immigration problems in Australia, writing pamphlets, testifying in 1845 before the House of Commons upon her return to England—which had used Australia as a dumping group for criminals, the insane and paupers—and organizing a more rational immigration system.

## Caroline Misses Australia

Caroline suffered in her old age from dropsy and a bad heart. Lying in her English bed, she missed Australia. She was not financially well off. Had she not been awarded a £100 pension, she and Archy might actually have suffered, for they had contributed large sums of their own money to charity.

A few days before her death in 1877, Caroline was able to partake of the sacrament of communion just as she had done before every major change in her life. She died of bronchitis late in March. Some English papers noted her passing, but the Australian papers did not note the event at all except to insert a notice that was paid for by her children.

 *Recommended reading: Mary Hoban,* Fifty-One Pieces of Wedding Cake: A Biography of Caroline Chisholm *(Kilmore, Victoria: Lowden Publishing, 1973).*

# "MISSION IMPOSSIBLE"

*B*ullets sprayed all around Gladys as she ran for her
life. She fell, and the bullets came nearer. The brave
*woman pulled off her thick, padded coat and rolled under a*
*bush, wadding up the coat as a shield against the bullets, which*
*riddled the coat. She jumped up and ran on, falling, running and crawling until at last the*
*pursuit ceased. After that she walked all day. The Japanese High Command in China had put*
*a reward of £100 on her capture, dead or alive.*

## A Youth with a Mission

Born in London, the daughter of a postman, Gladys's one desire was to be on the stage.

## Gladys Aylward

**Born:** Around 1902 in
London, England
**Education:** Failed out of
Inland Mission School
in England
**Married:** Did not marry
**Children:** None
**Died:** January 3, 1970, in
Taiwan
**Quote:** "Christians never
retreat!"

Although she had been raised to attend church, church services held little interest for her. Despite this, one day when she was a teenager, she attended a religious meeting and realized that God had a claim on her life. She accepted Jesus as her Savior, and while probably still in her teens, Gladys read a magazine article about China that changed her life. She kept thinking about the millions of people in that distant land who had not yet heard of God's love, and she knew she had to tell them.

She was informed that she would have to attend missionary training school first, which she did. After three months, the mission agency broke the news: She was not qualified for service in China.

Young Gladys couldn't accept that decision as final. She tried to serve God in other ministries,

*The feature film* Inn of the Sixth Happiness, *starring Ingrid Bergman, was based on the life of Gladys Aylward, a woman who could not understand the meaning of the word* no *when souls were at stake. Transformed by the call of China, she spared nothing to attain her dream.*

but her inner sense of calling to China continued to obsess her. She just had to go—even without a mission agency to send her. She began to save the meager wages she earned as a housemaid, confident that God would help her pay her way.

On Saturday, October 15, 1932, at the age of thirty, Gladys left the Liverpool station in London for the long train ride across Europe and Russia. Japan was at war with both Russia and China, and travel in that region was dangerous. Her trip included several narrow escapes in the middle of war zones.

In Vladivostock, her passport was taken from her, and for days Russian authorities refused to allow her to depart. In desperation, she boldly snatched her passport from the hand of the interpreter who had taken it and threw it behind her into her bedroom. "You are not coming in here," she said with a boldness she did not feel.

The interpreter declared himself her master, saying that he could do as he wished. "Oh no you cannot. You may not believe in God, but he is here. Touch me and see. Between you and me he has put a barrier. Go!"

Shivering, the man left. Gladys escaped to a Japanese vessel with the help of an old man and a girl. A few days later, she reached Yangchen, China, and took up work assisting a retired missionary lady at an inn for muleteers.

## An Impressive "Feet"

For centuries the Chinese had observed the practice of footbinding. From childhood, women's feet were bent and tightly wrapped to prevent normal growth. At about the time when Gladys reached China, the authorities were outlawing this practice, and the local magistrate appointed Gladys to the position of foot inspector, since she had normal feet. She used the opportunity to spread the Christian faith, and, as she had expected, God met her financial needs.

Gladys learned the Chinese language, a feat she called "one of God's great miracles." (The mission agencies had been sure that she lacked the intelligence for that.) Sharing the gospel in the villages around Yangchen, she began to take in unwanted children, and before long she had twenty little ones under her roof in addition to the thirty or forty wounded soldiers whom she cared for at any given time. The Chinese called her *"Ai-weh-deh,"* which means "Virtuous Woman."

## Trek to Safety

Over the years, the band of children she cared for grew to 100. Gladys adopted China as her homeland, becoming a citizen in 1936, and she even spied on the Japanese, who put out a bounty for her capture—dead or alive.

Should she leave? Praying, Gladys turned to the Bible. The first words her eyes fell on were "Flee ye, flee ye into the mountains." (see Genesis 19:17). So, she made up her mind to leave early the next morning. The Japanese came for her later that night.

The next day she fled, narrowly escaping the bullets of her pursuers. Her children, fortunately, were already in the village of Cheng Suen. Gladys met them there and decided to lead them into the province of Sian herself. She had been promised safety there by a friend, Madame Chiang.

The devoted missionary led her 100 children over the mountains on foot—a perilous journey of over 100 miles. After twenty-seven exhausting days and shivering nights, Gladys brought her children safely into Sian and collapsed.

How had she made it? The doctors were amazed at this woman, who was suffering from typhus, pneumonia, relapsing fever, malnutrition and extreme exhaustion.

Once Gladys had regained her strength, she resumed her ministry in this new region, sharing the gospel in the villages, in the prisons and among lepers.

Courtesy James S. Dennis, *Christian Missions and Social Progress* (New York: Fleming H. Revell, 1909)

*Sketches depicting the practice of footbinding*

## Burden for Britain

Gladys returned to Britain in 1947, not so much because of difficulties in China but because of a burden for the spiritual condition of her native country. She wrote, "England, seemingly so prosperous while other countries passed through terrible suffering at

*My heart is full of praise that one so insignificant, uneducated, and ordinary in every way could be used to His glory for the blessing of His people in poor persecuted China.*

*—Gladys Aylward*

the hands of Communist domination, had forgotten what was all important—the realization that God mattered in the life of a nation no less than in that of an individual."

After ten years in England, Gladys returned to Asia in 1955. Unable to settle on the Chinese mainland because of Communist rule, she established refugee centers in Hong Kong and Taipei. She ran an orphanage in Taiwan until her death in 1970. Throughout her years in China, her ministry was characterized by a humble dependence upon God in a steady stream of extreme circumstances.

*Recommended reading: Gladys Aylward, as told to Christine Hunter,* The Small Woman of the Inn of Sixth Happiness *(Chicago: Moody, 1970).*

# Part 9
## Beyond Motherhood

*They realized that God's
plan for them went beyond
raising their children.*

# EVERLASTING HAPPINESS

Courtesy Christian History Institute archives

"*Think of your mother, your brother, your aunt. Please, Perpetua, think of me, your aging father. But most of all, think of your little baby!*"

Perpetua agonized over the pain that she was causing her father and the sorrow of leaving her son to be raised by strangers. She and four others, including her slave Felicitas, were in jail in Carthage in North Africa. They were there because they were Christians.

It was around AD 200, and the Roman emperor Septimus Severus was cracking down on traitors. Christians showed a dangerous lack of loyalty to the empire; they wouldn't offer incense to the Roman gods—even under threat of death.

The Romans really didn't want martyrs, only a sacrifice to the official gods, a patriotic gesture. Surely this young woman, who came from a well-respected family, would see the sense of giving the sacrifice and complying. But Perpetua held firm. As a Christian, she felt that offering the required sacrifice was the same as denying that Jesus was her one and only Lord.

## Perpetua and Felicitas

**Born:** Unknown

**Education:** Perpetua was well educated

**Married:** Both married

**Children:** Both had one child

**Died:** Around 202 in Carthage

**Quote:** "My prison had suddenly become a palace." (Perpetua)

## Intense Pressure on New Mothers

Born into a well-to-do family, Perpetua was raised in or near Carthage. She was about twenty-two years old when she was arrested and had recently given birth to a son. She was an educated woman, fluent in Latin and Greek. Apparently she was a relatively new Christian too—she was actually baptized while in prison. Felicitas, her

*W*hat we know about Perpetua's prison experience comes from a diary that she kept. Other believers added the details of her execution. Hers is thought to be the first writing that we have by a Christian woman.

> After a few days we were taken into prison, and I was much afraid because I had never known such darkness. O bitter day! There was a great heat because of the press, there was cruel handling of the soldiers. Lastly I was tormented there by care for the child.
> —Perpetua

slave girl, was like a sister to her. She too was a new mother—she gave birth shortly after her arrest.

Perpetua's son was brought to her in the hope that her attachment to him would change her mind. After her baby was brought to her in the dungeon, she wrote, "All at once I regained my health, relieved of my worry and anxiety about the child. My prison had suddenly become a palace, so that I wanted to be there rather than anywhere else."

Young women, especially those from noble families, were expected to obey their fathers. Three times Perpetua's father was allowed in to beg her to change her mind. No decent daughter in their patriarchal society would cause her father public disgrace. But she stunned Roman society when she refused to renounce her faith.

Christianity had established a new family for her—the Church—and Perpetua's loyalty was to the Body of Christ and to her heavenly Father. This new loyalty superseded any obligations to her natural family or her human father. Supported by their new family, both Perpetua and Felicitas knew that their infants would be cared for.

The resolve of the two young women and their friends was unshakable. To deny Christ was worse than death for them. To follow Him was their first loyalty, no matter what the cost. Shortly before her trial, Perpetua received a series of visions from the Lord, reassuring her of His strength and presence.

## Perpetua and Felicitas Stand Firm

When the fatal day came, Perpetua and Felicitas left the prison for the arena "joyfully as though they were on their way to heaven," as an eyewitness account puts it. Before a raging crowd, the Christians were thrown to the wild beasts. A mad heifer charged the women and tossed them around, but Perpetua rose and helped Felicitas to her feet. She was ready, even eager, to die for the Lord. Her clothing had been ripped, so she modestly covered herself and asked if she could have a hairpin. She fixed her hair to avoid an unkempt appearance that might suggest that she was in mourning. "You must all stand fast in the faith and love one another," she called to the other martyrs, "and do not be weakened by what we have gone through!"

When the beasts failed to kill the women, soldiers came to finish them off. But the soldier who came to Perpetua was trembling so badly that he struck bone and hurt her so that she cried out. She had to guide the sword to her throat, which the crowd took as an indication that she was giving her life willingly.

Thus the two young women, new in the faith, quickly became heroines and examples for Christians everywhere. Two centuries later, Augustine pointed out the significance of the names of the two martyrs. Joined together, *perpetua felicitas* means "everlasting happiness," which is exactly what they received. Even today, believers can be inspired by their uncompromising faithfulness to the Lord.

*How could Perpetua, a Christian, have a slave? The fact is that Christianity did not immediately attack the institution of slavery. It did something more basic. The Church taught a new way of looking at all people—including slaves—as equally beloved and free in Christ, thereby undermining the foundation of slavery. Thus the two women acted as sisters to each other.*

*Recommended reading: Mark Reasoner, "The Martyrdom of Perpetua and Felicitas," http://www.bethel.edu/~letnie/African Christianity/WNAMartyrdomofPerpetua.html.*

# "THIS IS ALL WE HAVE LEFT"

Courtesy Mrs. Howard Taylor,
*The Triumph of John and Betty
Stam* (Philadelphia: China
Inland Mission, 1935)

O n December 6, 1934, Betty was bathing three-month-old Helen Priscilla Stam when Tsingteh's city magistrate appeared. Communist forces were near, he said, and he advised the Stams to flee. He himself hurried away.

For weeks now, similar rumors had spattered around them like uncertain rain, so Betty's husband, John, went out to investigate the situation for himself. He received conflicting reports. Taking no chances, they hired chairs and coolies to carry Betty and the baby to safety if need be.

Before the Stams could make their escape, however, the Communists were inside the city. By little-known paths, they had streamed over the mountains behind government troops. Now gunshots sounded in the streets and looting began. The coolies fled.

*Betty Stam*

**Born:** February 22, 1906, in Albion, MI
**Education:** Attended Moody Bible Institute
**Married:** John Stam on October 25, 1933
**Children:** One
**Died:** December 7, 1934, near Miaosheo, China
**Quote:** "Lord, here I am! Here, Lord, am I!"

A faithful cook and a maid had stayed behind with the Stams, and the missionary couple knelt with their servants in prayer. The Communists began to pound at their door. John opened it and spoke courteously to the four leaders who entered, asking them if they were hungry. Betty brought them tea and cakes. But the courtesy meant nothing. The leaders demanded all the money the Stams had, and John handed it over. As the men bound him, he pleaded for the safety of his wife and child. The Communists left Betty and Helen behind and led John off to their headquarters.

Before long, they reappeared to take Betty and her child. The maid and the cook pleaded to be allowed to accompany Betty. "No," barked the captors as they threatened to shoot.

Courtesy Lee S. Huienga, *John and Betty Stam* (Grand Rapids: Zondervan, 1935)

*John and Betty in Chinese garb*

*"It is better for you to stay here," Betty whispered. "If anything happens to us, look after the baby." Perhaps involuntarily she clutched Helen a little tighter. The Chinese called the infant "Ai-lien," "Love-link."*

*Betty was led to her husband's side. Little Helen needed some things, and John was allowed to return home under the supervision of guards to fetch them. But when he arrived, the cook and the maid reported that everything had been stolen. The two servants pleaded with the guards for the Stams' lives to no avail.*

*That night John was allowed to write a letter to mission authorities. "My wife, baby and myself are today in the hands of the Communists in the city of Tsingteh. Their demand is twenty thousand dollars for our release. . . . We were too late. The Lord bless and guide you. As for us, may God be glorified, whether by life or by death."*

*Prisoners in the local jail were released to make room for the Stams. Frightened by rifle fire, Helen cried out, and one of the Communists said, "Let's kill the baby. It is in our way."*

*A bystander asked, "Why kill her? What harm has she done?"*

*"Are you a Christian?" shouted one of the Reds.*

*The man said that he was not; he was one of the prisoners who had just been released. "Will you die for this foreign baby?" they asked him. As Betty hugged Helen to her chest, the man was hacked to pieces before her eyes.*

## Terror in the Streets

The next morning their captors led the Stams toward Miaosheo, twelve miles away. John carried little Helen, but Betty, who was not physically strong due to a youthful bout with inflammatory rheumatitis, was allowed to ride a horse part of the way.

Terror reigned in the streets of Miaosheo. Under guard, the foreign family was hustled into the postmaster's shop. "Where are you going?" asked the postmaster, who recognized them from their previous visits to his town.

"We do not know where they are going, but we are going to heaven," answered John. He left a letter with the postmaster. It was addressed to the mission board, and part of it said, "I tried to persuade them to let my wife and baby go back from Tsingteh with a letter to you, but they would not let her."

That night the three Americans were held in the house of a wealthy man who had fled. They were guarded by soldiers. John was tied to a post all that cold night, but Betty was allowed enough freedom to tend to the baby.

## Execution

The next morning the young couple were led through town without the baby. Their hands were tightly bound, and they were stripped of their outer garments as if they were common criminals. John walked barefoot, because he had given his socks to Betty. The Communists jeered and called the townsfolk to come see an execution. The terrified people obeyed.

*When we consecrate ourselves to God, we think we are making a great sacrifice, and doing lots for Him, when really we are only letting go some little, bitsie trinkets we have been grabbing, and when our hands are empty, He fills them full of His treasures.*

*—Elisabeth Scott Stam*

On the way to the execution, a medicine-seller who was considered a lukewarm Christian at best stepped from the crowd and pleaded for the lives of the two foreigners. The Communists angrily ordered him back, but the man would not be stilled. His house was searched, a Bible and a hymnbook were found, and he too was dragged away to die as a hated Christian.

John pleaded for the man's life. The Communist leader sharply ordered him to kneel, and as John was speaking softly, the leader swung his sword through the missionary's throat so that his head was severed from his body. Betty did not scream. She quivered and fell bound beside her husband's body. As she knelt there, the same sword ended her life with a single blow.

## Betty

Betty Scott, daughter of missionaries, was born in the United States but was reared in China. She went to the United States for missionary training and prepared to follow in her parents' footsteps. She would work in China or wherever else the Lord directed her. She thought He might want to use her talent with words, which she used to express her thoughts, which ranged from the serious to the bubbly, as can be seen in this brief

*Fittingly, in light of her end, Betty's life verse was "For me to live is Christ and to die is gain."*

excerpt from her poem "A Jingle of Words": "Don't you love the lively words—/ Flicker, leap and flash,/ Tumble, stumble, pitch and toss,/ Dive and dart and dash."

China proved to be in God's plan for Betty. At a prayer meeting for China, she met John Stam, and a friendship developed between them that ripened into love. They painfully recognized, however, that marriage was not yet possible. "The China Inland Mission has appealed for men, single men, to itinerate in sections where it would be impossible to take a woman until more settled work has commenced," wrote John. He committed the matter to the Lord, whose work, he felt, must come before any human affection. At any rate, Betty would be leaving for China before him to work in an entirely different region, and so they must be separated anyhow. As a matter of fact, John had not yet even been accepted by the China Inland Mission, whereas Betty had. They parted after a long, tender day of sharing their faith, picnicking, talking and praying.

Betty sailed to China while John continued his studies. On July 1, 1932, John too was accepted for service in China. Now at least he could head toward the same continent as Betty. He sailed for Shanghai.

Meanwhile, a senior missionary had been captured by the Communists in the region where Betty was to have worked. The mission directors decided to keep her in a temporary station, and later ill health brought her to Shanghai. Thus, without any effort on her part, she was in Shanghai when John landed in China. Immediately they became engaged, and a year later they were married, long before they had expected to be. In October of 1934 Helen Priscilla was born to them.

## Huddling in the Hills

For two days after the Stams' execution, local Christians huddled in hiding in the hills around Miaosheo. Among them was a Chinese evangelist named Mr. Lo. Through informants, he learned that the Communists had captured two foreigners. At first he did not realize that it was John and Betty Stam, with whom he had worked, but as he received more details, he put two and two together.

As soon as government troops entered the valley and it was safe to venture forth, he hurried to town. His questions were met with silence. Everyone was fearful that Communist spies might report anyone who said too much.

An old woman whispered to Pastor Lo that there was a baby left behind. She nodded in the direction of the mansion where John and Betty had been chained during their last night on earth. Pastor Lo hurried to the site and found room after room trashed by the bandits. Then he heard a muffled cry. Tucked by her mother into a little sleeping bag, Helen was warm and alive, although hungry after her two-day fast.

The kindly pastor took the child in his arms and carried her to his wife. With the help of a local Christian family, he wrapped the bodies that still lay upon the hillside and placed them into coffins. To the crowd that gathered he explained that the missionaries had only come to tell them how they might find forgiveness of sin in Christ. Leaving others to bury the dead, he hurried home. Somehow Helen had to be gotten to safety.

Courtesy Mrs. Howard Taylor, *The Triumph of John and Betty Stam* (Philadelphia: China Inland Mission, 1935)

*Pastor Lo, who rescued the baby*

Pastor Lo's own son, a boy of four, was desperately ill and semiconscious after days of exposure in the hills. Pastor Lo had to find a way to carry the children a hundred miles through mountains infested with bandits and Communists. Brave men were found who were willing to help bear the children to safety, but there was no money to pay them for their efforts. Pastor Lo had been robbed of everything he had.

But from beyond the grave, Betty provided. Tucked in Helen's sleeping bag were a change of clothes and some diapers. Pinned between these articles of clothing were two $5 bills, enough to pay for the men's assistance.

Placing the children in rice baskets slung from the two ends of a bamboo pole, the group departed quietly, taking turns carrying the precious cargo over their shoulders. Mrs. Lo was able to find Chinese mothers along the way who nursed Helen. On foot, they came safely through their perils. Pastor Lo's own boy recovered consciousness suddenly and sat up, singing a hymn.

## *"This Is All We Have Left"*

Eight days after the Stams fell into Communist hands, a missionary in Süancheng heard a rap at his door. He opened it and a Chinese woman, stained with travel, entered the house bearing a bundle in her arms. "This is all we have left," she said brokenly.

Courtesy Mrs. Howard Taylor, *The Triumph of John and Betty Stam* (Philadelphia: China Inland Mission, 1935)

*Helen Stam*

The missionary took the bundle and turned back the blanket to uncover the sleeping face of Helen Stam. Many kind hands had labored to preserve the infant girl, but none kinder than Betty's, who had spared no effort for her baby even as she herself faced degradation and death.

 *Recommended reading: Mrs. Howard Taylor,* The Triumph of John and Betty Stam *(Philadelphia: China Inland Mission, 1935).*

# Recommended Reading

**Editors' Note:** Many of the stories presented in this book have been used in previous Christian History Institute projects. The following list identifies resources that have been helpful in preparing *Great Women in Christian History*. We hope this will assist readers who want to do further exploration into the historical context and lasting influence of the women we have presented.

## Articles and Pamphlets

Chisholm, Caroline. "Female Immigration Considered in a Brief Account of the Sydney Immigrants' Home." London, 1842.

Christian History Institute. "The Letter of the Churches of Vienne and Lyons to the Churches of Asia and Phrygia Including the Story of the Blessed Blandina." Pocket Classics. Worcester, PA: Christian History Institute, 1994.

Dominican Sisters of Hawthorne. "The Dominican Sisters of Hawthorne." Fidelity: 1900-2000. Undated pamphlet.

*Glimpses of People, Events, Life and Faith from the Church across the Ages.* Worcester, PA: Christian History Institute, 1996.

King, Louis L. "Mother Whittemore's Miracles." *Alliance Witness.*

Kroeber. "Preventing Women from Being Born." *The Progressive* (December 1988).

Lathrop, Rose Hawthorne, ed. *Christ's Poor*, vols. 1-4. New York: St. Rose's Free Home, 1901.

Stowe, Harriet Beecher. "The Freeman's Dream." In *Uncle Sam's Emancipation: Earthly Care, A Heavenly Discipline, and Other Tales and Sketches* by Harriet Beecher Stowe. Freeport, NY: Books for Libraries, 1970.

Wilson, Katherina M. "Christian Women Writers of the Medieval World." *Christian History* 10, no. 2.

## Books

Anderson, Gerald H., ed. *Biographical Dictionary of Christian Missions.* New York: Macmillan Reference USA; London: Simon & Schuster and Prentice Hall International, 1998.

Augustine. *The Confessions of St. Augustine.* Translated by Rex Warner. New York: Mentor/Omega, 1963.

Aylward, Gladys, as told to Christine Hunter. *The Small Woman of the Inn of Sixth Happiness.* Chicago: Moody, 1970.

Bainton, Roland H. *Here I Stand: A Life of Martin Luther.* New York: Mentor, 1950.

Baseheart, Mary Catharine. *Person in the World: Introduction to the Philosophy of Edith Stein.* Dordrecth, Netherlands: Kluwer Academic, 1977.

Bentsen, Cheryl. *Masai Days.* New York: Simon and Schuster, 1989.

Bradford, Sarah H. *Harriet Tubman: The Moses of Her People.* New York: Geo. R. Lockwood & Son, 1886.

Brailsford, Mabel Richmond. *A Tale of Two Brothers: John and Charles Wesley.* New York: Oxford University Press, 1954.

Brawley, Benjamin Griffith. *Negro Builders and Heroes.* Chapel Hill, NC: University of North Carolina Press, 1937.

Bueltmann, A.J. *White Queen of the Cannibals: The Story of Mary Slessor.* Chicago: Moody, n.d.

Burger, Delores T. *Women Who Changed the Heart of the City: The Untold Story of the City Rescue Mission Movement.* Grand Rapids, MI: Kregel, 1997.

Butler, Alban. *Lives of the Saints.* Westminster, MD: Christian Classics, 1981.

Cable, Mildred and Francesca French. *Through Jade Gate and Central Asia: An Account of Journeys in Kansu, Turkestan and the Gobi Desert.* London: Hodder and Stoughton, 1939.

*The Catholic Encylopedia.* New York: Robert Appleton, 1914.

Christian, Carol and Gladys Plummer. *God and One Redhead: Mary Slessor of Calabar.* London: Hodder and Stoughton, 1970.

Conrad, Earl. *Harriet Tubman.* Washington, DC: Associated Publishers, 1943.

Cross, F.L. and E.A. Livingstone, eds. *The Oxford Dictionary of the Christian Church.* Oxford: Oxford University Press, 1997.

Daniel-Rops, Henri. *The Heroes of God: Eleven Courageous Men and Women Who Risked Everything to Spread the Catholic Faith.* Garden City, NY: Doubleday, 1959.

Davis, Rebecca Henry. *With Daring Faith: A Biography of Amy Carmichael.* Greenville, SC: Bob Jones University, 1987.

de Riencourt, Amaury. *Sex and Power in History.* New York: D. McKay, 1974.

de Robeck, Nesta. *St. Elizabeth of Hungary: A Study of Twenty-Four Years.* Milwaukee: Bruce Publishing, 1954.

Deen, Edith. *Great Women of the Christian Faith.* New York: Harper, 1956.

Delaney, John J., ed. *Saints for All Seasons.* Garden City, NY: Doubleday, 1978.

*Dictionary of American Biography.* New York: Scribner, 1958-1964.

Drijvers, Jan Willem. *Helena Augusta: The Mother of Constantine the Great and the Legend of Her Finding of the True Cross.* Leiden, NY: E.J. Brill, 1992.

Dyer, Helen S. *Pandita Ramabai: The Story of Her Life.* New York: Revell, 1911.

*Encyclopedia Americana.* New York: Americana, 1956.

*Encyclopedia of World Biography.* Detroit: Gale Research, 1998.

Eusebius. *The Ecclesiastical History.* Cambridge: Harvard University Press, 1959.

Evans, Mary J. *Women in the Bible: An Overview of All the Crucial Passages of Women's Roles.* Downers Grove, IL: InterVarsity, 1983.

Flanagan, Sabina. *Hildegard of Bingen, 1098-1179: A Visionary Life.* London: Routledge, 1989.

Foxe, John. *Foxe's Book of Martyrs.* Old Tappan, NJ: Fleming H. Revell, 1989.

Gerson, Noel B. *Harriet Beecher Stowe: A Biography.* New York: Praeger, 1976.

Gifford, Carolyn de Swarte. *Writing Out of My Heart: Selections from the Journal of Frances E. Willard, 1855-1896.* Urbana, IL: University of Illinois, 1995.

Gilder, George. *Men and Marriage.* Gretna, LA: Pelican, 1986.

Gillespie, Charles Coulston. *Dictionary of Scientific Biography.* New York: Scribner, 1970.

Goodwin, Grethe. *Anna Nitschmann, 1715-1760: Founder of the Moravian Single Sisters Choir.* Bethlehem, PA: Oaks Press, 1985.

Gordon, Anna Adams and Lady Henry Somerset. *The Beautiful Life of Frances E. Willard.* Chicago: WCTU, 1898.

Halasa, Malu. *Mary McLeod Bethune: Educator.* New York: Chelsea House, 1989.

Hanks, Geoffrey. *Friend of Prisoners: The Story of Elizabeth Fry.* Exeter, England: Pergamon, 1981.

Hart, James D. *The Oxford Companion to American Literature*. New York: Oxford University Press, 1965.

Hedrick, Joan D. *Harriet Beecher Stowe: A Life*. New York: Oxford University Press, 1994.

Hege, Ruth. *We Two Alone: Attack and Rescue in the Congo*. Greenville, SC: Emerald House, 1997.

Herbstrith, Waltraud. *Edith Stein: A Biography*. San Francisco: Harper and Row, 1971.

*Heroes of the Cross: Pandita Ramabai, Mary Slessor, Rasalama and Heroes in Madagascar*. London: Marshall, Morgan & Scott, 1933.

Hildegard of Bingen. *The Letters of Hildegard of Bingen*. Translated by Joseph L. Baird and Radd K. Ehrman. New York: Oxford University Press, 1994.

Hine, Darlene Clark, ed. *Black Women in America*. Brooklyn, NY: Carlson, 1993.

Hoban, Mary. *Fifty-One Pieces of Wedding Cake: A Biography of Caroline Chisholm*. Kilmore, Victoria: Lowden Publishing, 1973.

Holder, Mig. *Mary Jones and Her Bible*. Swindon, UK: Bible Society [The British and Foreign Bible Society], 1992.

Hopkins, Mary Alden. *Hannah More and Her Circle*. New York: Longman, Green, 1947.

Houghton, Frank L. *Amy Carmichael of Dohnavur: The Story of a Lover and Her Beloved*. Fort Washington, PA: Christian Literature Crusade, n.d.

Huizenga, Lee S. *John and Betty Stam, Martyrs*. Grand Rapids, MI: Zondervan, 1935.

James, Edward T., ed. *Notable American Women, 1607-1950: A Biographical Dictionary*. Cambridge, MA: Belknap, 1971.

Jeffrey, Mary Pauline. *Ida S. Scudder of Vellore: The Life Story of Ida Sophia Scudder*. Mysore, India: J. Brown, 1951.

Johnson, Paul. *A History of Christianity*. New York: Touchstone, 1979.

Johnston, Johanna. *Runaway to Heaven: The Story of Harriet Beecher Stowe*. Garden City, NY: Doubleday, 1963.

Joseph, Sister M., O.P. *Out of Many Hearts: Mother M. Alphonsa Lathrop and Her Work*. Hawthorne, NY: Servants for the Relief of Incurable Cancer, 1965.

Kennedy, D. James and Jerry Newcombe. *What If Jesus Had Never Been Born?* Nashville: Thomas Nelson, 1994.

Kent, John. *Elizabeth Fry.* New York: Arco, 1963.

Keyes, Francis Parkinson. *The Cost of a Bestseller.* New York: Messner, 1950.

Knight, Helen C. *Lady Huntington and Her Friends.* New York: American Tract Society, 1853.

Kunitz, Stanley J. and Howard Haycraft, *American Authors 1600-1900: A Biographical Dictionary of American Literature.* New York: H.W. Wilson, 1977.

Livingstone, W.P. *Christina Forsyth of Fingoland.* New York: George H. Doran, 1919.

———. *Mary Slessor of Calabar: Pioneer Missionary.* London: Hodder and Stoughton, 1917.

Lyons, Albert S. and R. Joseph Petrucelli. *Medicine: An Illustrated History.* New York: Henry N. Abrams, 1987.

MacNicol, Nicol. *Pandita Ramabai: A Builder of Modern India.* Calcutta, India: Associated Press, 1926. Reprinted in *What Liberates a Woman?* by Vishal Mangalwadi. New Delhi: Nivedit Good Books, 1996.

Magnunson, Norris. *Salvation in the Slums: Evangelical Social Work, 1865-1920.* Grand Rapids, MI: Baker Book House, 1977.

McNeill, John. *Illustrated Lives of the Saints.* New York: Crescent Books, 1995.

McReynolds, Kathy. *Susanna Wesley: The Godly Mother of Two of Christianity's Most Gifted Men—John and Charles Wesley.* Minneapolis: Bethany House, 1998.

More, Hannah. *The Shepherd of Salisbury Plain.* New York: American Tract Society, between 1827 and 1833.

Moreau, A. Scott. *Evangelical Dictionary of World Missions.* Grand Rapids, MI: Baker Books, 2000.

Neill, Stephen, Gerald H. Anderson and John Goodwin. *Concise Dictionary of the Christian World Mission.* Nashville: Abingdon Press, 1971.

———. *A History of Christian Missions.* Great Britain: Pelican, 1964.

*New Catholic Encyclopedia.* New York: McGraw-Hill, 1967.

Oben, Freda Mary. *Edith Stein: Scholar, Feminist, Saint.* New York: Alba House, 1988.

Peterson, William J. *Harriet Beecher Stowe Had a Husband.* Wheaton, IL: Tyndale, 1983.

———. *Martin Luther Had a Wife.* Wheaton, IL: Tyndale, 1983.

Piercy, Josephine K. *Anne Bradstreet.* New York: Twayne Publishers, 1965.

Platt, W.J. *Three Women: Mildred Cable, Francesca French, Evangeline French*. London: Hodder and Stoughton, 1964.

Pollard, Arthur, gen. ed. *Webster's New World Companion to English and American Literature*. New York: Popular Library, 1976.

Ruffin, Bernard. *Fanny Crosby: The Hymn Writer*. Cleveland, OH: United Church Press, 1976.

Schlenther, Boyd Stanley. *Queen of the Methodists: The Countess of Huntingdon and the Eighteenth-Century Crisis of Faith and Society*. Durham, England: Durham Academic, 1997.

Seymour, Aaron Crossley Hobart. *The Life and Times of Selina, Countess of Huntingdon*. London: W.E. Painter, 1844.

Singer, Charles. *A Short History of Scientific Idea to 1900*. London: Oxford University Press, 1959.

Smith, Amanda. *An Autobiography: The Story of the Lord's Dealings with Mrs. Amanda Smith, the Colored Evangelist*. New York: Oxford University Press, 1987.

Stagg, Evelyn and Frank. *Woman in the World of Jesus*. Louisville: Westminster John Knox, 1978.

Stein, Edith. *Edith Stein: Self-Portrait In Letters, 1916-1942*. Translated by Josephine Koeppel. Washington, DC: Institute of Carmelite Studies, 1994.

Stephen, Leslie and Sidney Lee, eds. *The Dictionary of National Biography*. London: Oxford University Press, 1921-1996.

Stowe, Charles Edward and Lyman Beecher Stowe. *Harriet Beecher Stowe: The Story of Her Life*. Boston: Houghton Mifflin, 1911.

Stowe, Harriet Beecher. *Uncle Tom's Cabin*. Seacaucus, NJ: Longriver, 1976.

Strachey, Ray. *Frances Willard: Her Life and Work*. London: F. Fisher Unwin, 1912.

Tada, Joni Eareckson. *Joni: An Unforgettable Story*. Grand Rapids, MI: Zondervan, 2001.

Taylor, Mrs. Howard. *The Triumph of John and Betty Stam*. Philadelphia: China Inland Mission, 1935.

Tucker, Ruth A. *Daughters of the Church: Women and Ministry from New Testament Times to the Present*. Grand Rapids, MI: Academie Books, 1987.

——. *Guardians of the Great Commission: The Story of Women in Modern Missions*. Grand Rapids, MI: Academie Books, 1988.

Uglow, Jennifer, comp. and ed. *Continuum Dictionary of Women's Biography.* London: Macmillan, 1989.

Walsh, James J. *Mother Alphonsa: Rose Hawthorne Lathrop.* New York: Macmillan, 1930.

———. *Old Time Makers of Medicine.* New York: Fordham University, 1911.

Welch, Edwin. *Spiritual Pilgrim: A Reassessment of the Life of the Countess of Huntingdon.* Cardiff: University of Wales, 1995.

White, Elizabeth Wade. *Anne Bradstreet: The Tenth Muse.* New York: Oxford University Press, 1971.

Whiting, Lilian. *Women Who Have Ennobled Life.* Philadelphia: Union, 1915.

Whittemore, Emma M. *Records of Modern Miracles.* Edited by F.A. Robinson. Toronto, Ontario: Missions of Biblical Education, 1947.

Wilson, Dorothy Clarke. *Dr. Ida: The Story of Dr. Ida Scudder of Vellore.* New York: McGraw-Hill, 1959.

———. *Granny Brand: Her Story.* New York: Christian Herald Books, 1976.

Wintle, Justin. *Makers of 19th Century Culture, 1800-1914.* London: Routledge and Kegan Paul, 1982.

Woodbridge, John, gen. ed. *More Than Conquerors: Portraits of Believers from All Walks of Life.* Chicago: Moody, 1992.

Yost, Edna. *American Women of Science.* Philadelphia: Lippincott, 1955.

## Web Sites

Christian Medical College. "Ida S. Scudder." http://cmch-vellore.edu/htm/scudder.htm.

Cook, Faith. "Selina, Countess of Huntingdon." Evangelicaltimes.org (October 2001). http://www.evangelical-times.org/articles/oct01/oct01a11.htm.

"Elizabeth Fry." http://www.spartacus.schoolnet.co.uk/REfry.htm.

"Frances Jane Crosby, 1820-1915." Believersweb.org (March 13, 2003). http://www.believersweb.org/view.cfm?ID=83.

"How It All Began: The Mary Jones Story." The Bible Cause. http://www.biblesociety.ca/bible_cause/how_began/mary_jones.html.

"In the Radiance of Anne Marie Javouhey." Cluny in the Caribbean.org. http://www.
   clunycarib.org/spirituality.htm.

"The Life and Works of Hildegard von Bingen (1098-1179)." http://www.fordham.
   edu/halsall/med/hildegarde.html.

"Mary Slessor 1848-1915: 'Mother of All the Peoples.' " http://www.dundeecity.gov.uk/
   centlib/slessor/mary.htm.

"Missionary and Feminist Icon." Christianityandrenewal.com. http://www.christianity
   andrenewal.com/archdec2001d.htm.

Reasoner, Mark. "The Martyrdom of Perpetua and Felicitas." African Christianity.
   http://www.bethel.edu/~letnie/AfricanChristianity/WNAMartyrdomofPerpetua.
   html.

Smithers, David. "Pandita Ramabai: Prayer Makes History." The Watchword. http://
   www.watchword.org/smithers/ww45a.html.

"St. Perpetua: The Passion of Saints Perpetua and Felicity." Internet Medieval Source
   Book. http://www.fordham.edu/halsall/source/perpetua.html.